WHEN THE CONFLICT ENDS, WHAT THEN?

HUMAN DESTINY WEIGHED IN THE BALANCES OF TIME

BY CARL H. WATERS

TEACH Services, Inc.
PUBLISHING
www.TEACHServices.com • (800) 367-1844

World rights reserved. This book or any portion thereof may not be copied or reproduced in any form or manner whatever, except as provided by law, without the written permission of the publisher, except by a reviewer who may quote brief passages in a review.

The author assumes full responsibility for the editing of and accuracy of all facts and quotations as cited in this book. The opinions expressed in this book are the author's personal views and interpretations, and do not necessarily reflect those of the publisher.

This book is provided with the understanding that the publisher is not engaged in giving spiritual, legal, medical, or other professional advice. If authoritative advice is needed, the reader should seek the counsel of a competent professional.

Copyright © 2023 Carl H. Waters
Copyright © 2023 TEACH Services, Inc.
ISBN-13: 978-1-4796-1522-3 (Paperback)
ISBN-13: 978-1-4796-1523-0 (ePub)
Library of Congress Control Number: 2022920936

All Scripture is from the King James Version of the Holy Scriptures.

DEDICATION

I dedicate these studies to my precious children:

Adrienne   Always

Andrea   Anticipate

Aaron   Angels

Wendy   Watching

Anthony   And they do

Andrew   Admirably

Whom Jesus has given to my adorable wife, Aryonna, and me to gently lead by love in the pathway that leads to the throne of God by making the principles of Christ's Kingdom their own that they may know Him whom to know is eternal life. May God so imbue you with His Spirit and grant you knowledge and understanding according to His plan for your redemption that, through His wisdom, power, & love, Christ be manifest in you, the hope of glory. The faith of Jesus says, Amen!

TABLE OF CONTENTS

I	A Scriptural Outline of Human History	7
II	Biblical Principles of Interpretation	11
III	The Great Controversy - Creation to the Flood	17
IV	The Great Controversy - The Seed of the Serpent	22
V	The Great Controversy - The Seed of the Woman	29
VI	Daniel 2 - Rise & Fall of Pagan Universal Empires	39
VII	Daniel 3 - Sun Worship - The Image & The Death Decree	46
VIII	Daniel 7 Part 1 - Attributes of the Universal Empires	51
IX	Daniel 7 Part 2 - The Papacy & Judgment, Judgment, & Judgment	56
X	Revelation 12 - Paganism & The Early Christian Church	64
XI	Revelation 13 - Antichrist - The Leopard Beast - Paganism Cloaked in Garments of Christianity	71
XII	Daniel 8 - Paganism & The Papacy Trampling Upon The Sanctuary	77
XII	What Is & Why The Sanctuary?	85
XIV	The Sanctuary Ministry in The Holy Place	92
XV	The Sanctuary Ministry in The Most Holy Place	100
XVI	Daniel 9 - When God's Face Shines Upon The Sanctuary, The Shadow Meets The Substance That Cast The Shadow	107
XVII	Daniel 10 & 11 - Primary Kings of Persia & Greece - The King of The North & The King of The South	116

XVIII	Daniel 11 Part 2 - History Of The Roman Empire To The 1st Advent Of Christ	122
XIX	Daniel 11 Part 3 - Rome & Israel Until The Rise Of The Papacy	125
XX	Daniel 11 Part 4 -1260 Years Of Papal Supremacy & The Reformation	131
XXI	Daniel 11 Part 5 - Spiritual Babylon Vs Atheism, The Final Conflicts Between The Kings Of The North & The South	136
XXII	Daniel 11 Part 6 - Spiritual Babylon Pursuing World Dominance & Worship Encounters Spiritual Israel, & The Church Triumphs	146
XXIII	Daniel 12 Part 1 - The Climax, Events Surrounding Christ's 2nd Advent	156
XXIV	Daniel 12 Part 2 - A Sealed Book Until The Time Of The End	162
References		167

Chapter I

A SCRIPTURAL OUTLINE OF HUMAN HISTORY

I. **Antediluvian (Pre Flood)** — Creation to the Flood Gen 1-7
God's Representatives — The Patriarchs Adam to Noah.

II. **Post Diluvian (Post Flood)** — After the Flood to Mt Sinai Gen 8 to Ex 19
God's Representatives — The Patriarchs Shem to 12 tribes of Israel (Jacob)

III. **Period for Israels National Sovereignty** — Mt Sinai to Babylonian Captivity Ex 19:1-6 to 2 Chron 36:17-21, Deut 28:1-14, Jer 25:9-14
God's Representatives — National Israel: Theocracy to a Kingdom. Deut 17:14-20, 1Sam 8

IV. **Period for Sovereignty of the Pagan Empires** — Babylon to Rome Deut 28:15-66, Eze 21:24-27, Dan 2, 7-11:31
God's Representatives — Jews to Early Christian Church

V. **Period of the Divided Nations and Papal Supremacy** — Dark Ages & Papal Supremacy Dan 7:19-27, 8:9-14, 11:31-40, Rev 13:1-10, 2 Thes 2:1-12
God's Representatives — Christian Church in the Wilderness to Protestant Reform Churches

VI. Period of Divided Nations	Protestant Reformation to Advent
The Rise of the USA	Awakening. Rev 13:10, 11, 14:1-8,
	Dan 11:40-44, Rev 12:17, 19:10
God's Representatives	Protestant Reform Churches to
	Protestant Church of Rev 12:17
VII. Period - Divided Nations & a	A Restored Papacy & Her Image
Movement toward a New One	Rev 13:11-18, 8, 14:9-20
World Order to Christ Return	Rev 15-18, Dan 11:44, 45,
God's Representatives	Protestant Church of Rev 12:17 to
	144000 of Rev 7:1-8; 14:1-5

How God Is To Be Approached During During Human History

Throughout human history, God has always had a 'way' by which He was to be approached for worship, guidance, deliverance, and other redemptive needs. This "way" has specific and direct reference to Christ - "I am the way" (John 14:6).

In types and symbols, in feast and celebrations, Christ is represented as the only way to God (John 14:6), to rest (Matt 11:28, 29), to eternal life (1 John 5:11, 12), to wisdom, righteousness, sanctification, and redemption (1 Cor 1:30), to peace (John 14:27; 16:33), to love (1 John 4:7, 8), to victory (1 John 5:4, 5). This "way" was made a living reality by Christ's Substitutionary Holy Life and Sacrificial Death, by His Triumphant Resurrection and Glorious Ascension, by His Triumphal entry into the heavenly sanctuary to minister as our Great High Priest (Heb 9:11-14, 24).

> I. **In the Antediluvian and Post Diluvian Periods after the Fall, God was to be approached by "way" of "the sacrifice of the whole burnt offering,"** which pointed forward to the promised Messiah, who would come and offer Himself a sacrifice as mankind's substitute and surety of deliverance from sin. Gen 3:15, 4:3-7, 22:1-14

When God delivered Israel out of Egyptian bondage and brought them unto Himself at Mount Sinai, He made them an extension of His government upon the earth and inducted them into His church which is in Heaven. In giving them His 10 Commandment Law, God established Israel as a nation to be governed by the rule of law. In giving them the "earthly sanctuary," God gave Israel a more elaborate "way" by which He was to be approached, which provided a greater revelation of His plan for human redemption.

II. **During the periods for Israels national sovereignty** and the sovereignty of the pagan empires, **God revealed that His nations were to be governed by the rule of law and that He was to be approached by "way" of "the earthly sanctuary" with its animal sacrifices and ceremonial laws,** which included the sacrifice of the whole burnt offering.
Ex 19:1-6, 20:1-17, 25:8,9, Deut 17:14-20, Ezek 21:24-27

During the reign of Rome, the last pagan empire into whose hands God gave the sovereignty of the earth, the Messiah (the Christ) was born. After 33 years of the human experience Christ offered Himself as the sacrificial Lamb of God. When this occurred, type met anti-type, and the shadow met the substance that cast the shadow. The veil of the temple was rent from top to bottom indicating that God was no longer be approached by 'way' of "the earthly sanctuary" with its animal sacrifices and ceremonial laws.' Following this event, the 490 years cut from the 2300 years and made specifically applicable to the Jews, expired in AD 34 with the stoning of Steven, and literal Israel gave place to Spiritual Israel (the Christian Church) as God's agents for the spreading of the gospel (Dan 9:24-27, Acts 7:54 - 8:4, 9:1-16, 11:19-26, 13:42-48).

III. **From AD 34 to 1844, through the two periods of the divided nations - papal supremacy and the rise of the United States of America - God was to be approached by "way" of "Christ priesthood and ministry in the holy place of the Heavenly Sanctuary,"** where He pleads the blood of His sacrifice in behalf of believing, repentant sinners, and offers to them His holy life, generated in 33 years of the human experience, in exchange for their forfeited lives which He took to the cross.
Matt 27:50-54, 28:1-7, Acts 1:1-3, 9-11, Heb 8:1- 6, 9:11-14, 10:4-10, 12

Once God guided His people to discover in His Word that salvation is by faith in Christ Jesus alone, He marched them out of the darkness of the superstition, error, tradition, customs, and falsehood of Romanism. As the time approached for the fulfillment of the 2300 day/year prophecy - God sent advancing light to move His people forward in the reformation - to the Advent Awakening. However, the majority of the descendants of those whom the Lord had marched out of the darkness of Romanism had settled into denominations, ceased to reform, and were caught up in the industrial revolution.

    IV. During the Advent Awakening God cleaved out unto Himself a people to whom He could commit the last message of warning to be given to the world to usher in Christ 2nd Advent. **With the termination of the 2300 day/year prophecy in 1844, Christ past from the holy to the most holy place of the Heavenly Sanctuary to carry forward His final work of atonement.** He closed the door of ministration in the apartment where He had been approached since AD 34, and opened another door to the most holy apartment for the ministration of judgement and the blotting out of sins. **This is the seventh and final period of human history, described as "the Antitypical Day of Atonement," the period during which Christ is to be approach by "way" of "His ministry in the most holy place of the Heavenly Sanctuary."** When He ceases this ministry every case will have been decided for eternal life or eternal damnation, and human probation will close.

Then will come the time of trouble followed by God's execution of judgment and Christ's second advent to rescue His faithful followers from the hands of the wicked (Dan 7:7-14; 8:9-14; Acts 3:19-21; Rev 3:7, 8; 11:19; 20:11-15; 21:6-8; Rev 22:10-15).

Chapter II

BIBLICAL PRINCIPLES OF INTERPRETATION

Everything that God created was created under law - laws that govern the physical (natural) and the spiritual realms, laws that govern the nature of the thing created. As in the natural world, so in the spiritual world - success comes to those who discover and order their lives in harmony with these laws of God, and failure to those who disregard them.

Only free moral beings, possessing intellect, reason, will, and heart, and made in the image and likeness of God were created under moral law - the rule of right conduct and absolute principles defining the criterion of right action - what is true, honest, just, noble, virtuous, decent, pure, holy, righteous, and good. These principles are rooted and grounded in love, which is the ruling, foundational principle of the government of God and the chief and defining attribute of the very nature and character of God.

As such, inherent in the Word of God that called into being that which was not, are the laws that enable, uphold, sustain, govern, and promote the very existence of God's creation, providing stability, reliability, continuity and dependability Psalms 33:6 & 9

There are **principles, or laws, that govern the "rightly dividing the word of truth," "line upon line, precept upon precept."** 2 Tim 2:15 & Isa 28:9, 10

The Bible is spiritually inspired and constructed, written upon certain principles of interpretation. 2 Pet 1:19-21, John 14:15-17, 26, 1 Cor 2:9-14

Bible Typologies:

I. When the Godhead made plans for the creation of worlds, the Universe was an empty vacuum, enveloped in darkness. Because God is a personal

being, it was decided that the Son would be the visible manifestation of the Godhead. In the creation of worlds and and all that is in them, the Father willed, the Son generated, and the Spirit moved out to effect. **The Bible reveals the principle that the literal interpretation of Scripture is applicable when and where the Son's presence is manifested.**
Isa 59:1, 2, 15, 16, 19, 20, John 3:16, 17, 1 Cor 8:6, Col 1:12-19, 2:9.

A. On earth, before the fall of man, when Adam & Eve had open communion with their Maker, the Son of God.
B. On earth, after the fall, the Son of God stepped into the gulf that sin caused between God and man. In the events from the fall to His first advent, the Son mediated between God and man visibly, audibly, and physically, and manifested Himself to His followers in power, in glory, and finally in humility.
C. In heaven, after the resurrection and ascension, and subsequent termination of the 70 week prophecy of Dan 9:24, Christ mediates as our High Priest, and He sends to us His Spirit as His representative on the earth. While Christ is ministering in heaven, the things of the kingdom of grace are based upon the spiritual. Thus, things relating to Israel on earth must be interpreted to be:
   1. Literal up to the events surrounding the 70 week prophecy of Dan 9:24 which brought us to the Messiah, and ended in AD 34
   2. Spiritual from AD 34 to Christ's second advent.
   3. Literal after Christ's second advent

In keeping with his work of deception, Satan has counterfeited all that is true. Papal Rome, which rose to power in AD 538, is Satan's counterfeit of the ministry and kingdom of Christ. She fosters a system of interpretation that literalizes the prophecies concerning Palestine and Israel regarding the final conflict between Christ and Satan, and between the Church and her enemies. Indeed, the whole Roman Catholic system is based on applying literally the things of literal Israel while Christ is in Heaven. CTAM.

Thus, the literal king (pope), literal throne, literal bread, literal robes, literal candles, literal incense, literal earthly sanctuary, literal interpretation of prophecies pertaining to Israel and the Antichrist, and the literal Palestinian Armageddon are all counterfeits of those things which are spiritually applied to the New Testament in connection with Spiritual Israel.

II. **The Old Testament (OT) literal, national things pertaining to Israel and her enemies have their spiritual world wide application in connection with the church, Spiritual Israel, and her enemies.**
I Cor 10:6, 11, Rom 15:4, Heb 8:1-6, 9:1-9, 23, 24, 10:1-10, 12-18, CTAM
   A. **OT types of historical events, enacted in Palestine, were acted out parables, literal foreshadowings of things to come.**
   AA 583-586, DA 23, 77, CTAM
   B. NT writers used the phraseology pertaining to national Israel when writing about Spiritual Israel. OT terminology is now employed in a spiritual world wide sense in connection with the church.
   Rom 2:28,29, 9:6-9, Gal 3:29, Rev 7:4-8
   C. Spiritual Israel has inherited all the promises and blessings assured to literal, national Israel. **All the prophecies and promises which failed of meeting their redemptive fulfillment in literal national Israel will be fulfilled in spiritual worldwide Israel, the Christian church.** CTAM

III. **Messages emanating from God are built upon the past.** A movement today must look to the past for its support. Prophets in the past must have foretold its rise. 2 Pet 1:19-21, 1 Cor 14:32, 33, CTAM
   A. The past is thus seen to be a prophecy of the future. Ecc 3:14,15
   B. **The past experiences of God's people forms the foundation for understanding the present and future experiences and consummated hope of His Christian church.**
   C. In poetic language, the New and the Old Testaments shed light upon each other: (CTAM)
   The New is in the Old contained; the Old is by the New explained
   The New is latent in the Old; the Old is patent in the New
   The New is in the Old concealed; the Old is in the New revealed
   The New is in the Old enfolded; the Old is in the New unfolded
   D. A test of true doctrine is in its agreement with the rest of the Word of God. 1 Cor 14:32, 33, Isa 8:20 **God inspired movements do not destroy the foundations of the past.** Matt 5:17

IV. The Principle of the Double Application, the 1st and Last Mention.
   1 Cor 15:46
   A. **The first fulfillment is the natural; the last mention application is worldwide when applied to nations as nations, and worldwide and spiritual when applied to the Church and her enemies.**

1. In Matt 24, Luke 19:41-44, 21:20-24 instruction is given to God's people on when to occupy and when to flee that they may be delivered from the coming judgments by applying this principle.
B. The prophecies of Daniel are designed upon this principle: **The literal, national, local which are first mentioned provide the imagery applicable to worldwide, Spiritual Israel and her enemies at the end of the prophecies.** CTAM
   1. As Dan 1 describes literal Babylon's attack upon Literal Israel, her city and temple; so Dan 11:40-12:1 brings us to the final attack to be made by Spiritual Babylon upon Spiritual Israel
   2. Dan 2 & 7 begin with the activity of Literal Babylon and end with the activity of Spiritual Babylon.
   3. Dan 3 reveals in the experience of the 3 Hebrews the final struggle of Spiritual Israel when Spiritual Babylon endeavors to force all to worship her spiritual image. See Rev 13
   4. **The 2300 year prophecy** of Dan 8 concerning the restoration of the sanctuary **begins with the restoration of the earthly sanctuary** following the end of Jeremiah's prophecy of the 70 years for Jerusalems desolation - Jer 25:8-12, 29:10-14, Dan 9:1-19, Ezra 6:14, 15. It **ends with the restoration of the Heavenly Sanctuary.** Dan 8:13,14, Rev 11:1, 2, Isa 58:1-14

V. **The Bible contains much repetition, for by the principle of enlargement through repetition the Divine Teacher increases our understanding.** CTAM
   A. "For God speaketh once, yea twice, yet man perceiveth it not." Job 33:14, Ps 62:11
   B. By the crescendo plan earlier books lay the foundation for later books. The details accumulate until like an artist dipping his brush in different colors, a complete picture is produced.
      1. This principle is employed by God in creation and redemption. In both, He moves from the lower to the higher, from the material to the spiritual, from the earthly to the heavenly
      2. The prophecies which follow Dan 2 are but the enlargement of this foundational prophecy. Tracing human history from the rise and fall of universal empires following the carrying away of the Jews into Babylonian captivity, Dan 7, Dan 8 & 9, and Dan 10-12 successively enlarges upon the previous prophecy giving additional details, light, and truth.

3. The Revelation also exhibits this principle. Containing about 550 references to OT passages it is the consummation of all preceding books, which meet and end in the Revelation.
The Revelation repeats the past in prophesying the future.
The past is repeated but enlarged upon.

> By the crescendo plan earlier books lay the foundation for later books. The details accumulate until like an artist dipping his brush in different colors, a complete picture is produced.

What unique element of truth runs like a thread through these principles of interpretation?
- The literal, national, local versus the spiritual, international, worldwide. 1 Cor 10:1-6
- The seen, temporal, earthly versus the unseen, eternal, heavenly.
- Type versus antitype. 1 Cor 10:11
- The past versus the future. Ecc 3:14, 15
- The first mention versus the last mention. 1 Cor 15:45, 46

The former is a prophecy of the latter and the latter a revelation of the fulfillment of the former, unfolding events in their order over time. This is what is called A Typology.

A typology is the study and interpretation of signs, types, and symbols in the Bible that focuses on actual persons, places, events, and experiences of the Old Testament that are founded in a historical reality, but that points to a greater reality in the future New Testament times.

Thus the historicist approach to biblical interpretation is God's method versus the preterits view which tends to lock certain prophetic events in the past, or the futurist view which makes a miraculous leap in time to place certain events in the future.

God's method unfolds events over time so as to cast the spotlight upon the past, the present, and the future, revealing the triumphant issues in the great controversy between Christ and Satan that we may know where we are in the stream of time and what we must do to prepare for the crisis before us.

We have nothing to fear for the future, except as we shall forget how God has led in the past! (Life Sketches of Ellen G. White, page 196)

VI. Finally, the manner in which we approach the Scriptures will determine who will be by our side to influence our understanding. Therefore above all else, we should pray and entreat the Lord for the indwelling of His Spirit to lead and guide us into the truth as it is in Jesus. John 14:16, 26, 16:12-14, 1 Cor 2:9-15, Rom 8:1-10, 14

Chapter III

THE GREAT CONTROVERSY CREATION TO THE FLOOD

I. **From Creation to the Fall and the cancer of sin!**
   A. Genesis means "the origin or the beginning of the existence of." The book of Genesis opens with the divine declaration "In the beginning God created." If it stopped here one might conclude that chapter 1 is about the Genesis of the Universe. But the statement is specific in declaring "In the beginning God created the heaven and the earth." What follows is an exposition of what this means as God delineates the creation of a world to be the habitation and domain of the free moral beings, human beings, with whom He desires to share the boundless resources of His omnipotence in a relationship of love. This is the only account we have of God creating a world: Hence it may serves as a model of what God did in the creation of worlds. There is only one closed system that fits the model described in Genesis 1, a galaxy. Thus, we conclude the Genesis account to be the description of the creation of the Milky Way Galaxy. Astronomers say that there are 100 to 200 billion galaxies in the Universe. One can only imagine the number of worlds that the Godhead has created! Gen 1, Heb 1:1, 2
   1. All that the Lord created in 6 literal days was a perfect reflection of the wisdom, the power, the glory, the goodness, & love of the Creator, consistent with His mind, character, and personality - in perfect harmony and accord - in a state of rest within His will. However, God added the 7th Day to His creation as a sign and

seal of His finished work, a memorial of that state of rest, to be celebrated every 7 days. **The number 7 reveals the full, complete, perfect, and finished activity of God.** Gen 2:1-3

2. Written on the principle of enlargement through repetition, Chapter 2 gives greater details concerning the creation of man - male and female. **The Father willed, the Son generated, and the Spirit energized and indwelled the man, and he became a living soul**. Then, the woman was made from a rib taken from the man, and given to the man in the first marriage. Afterwards, God planted a garden home for the man and woman. It was here that the test of their loyalty to God - their Great Benefactor, took place. It is here that we learn of sins introduction into God's perfect universe before this world was created.

1 Cor 8:6, John 14:16, 17, Zech 4:6, Gen 2:9, 15-17, Heb 2:6-9

B. Not on the outskirts of the Universe, but **in the very presence of the Sovereign of the Universe Himself, sin raised its ugly head** among the highest order of created free moral beings, the angels.

1. **In whom did sin and evil have their beginning?**

   a. **Lucifer, the anointed covering cherub, the illuminated one, the son of the morning.** Eze 28:12-21, Isa 14:12-15, 1 John 3:8

   b. He did not foresee that attacking the Creator would be an attack upon creation and an attack upon the very laws that enable, uphold, sustain, govern, and promote everything created, including his very existence. Nor did he see that it was an attack upon the perfect accord, harmony, and rest that heretofore existed. **This mighty angel** upon whom God bestowed great gifts and talents, who occupied the very highest position of the angelic host, **entered into open rebellion against his LORD and Maker and led a third of the angels in following him until there was war in heaven** (Rev 12:3-9).

   c. When Christ was on earth He declared in whom sin had its beginning. 1 John 3:8, Heb 2:14, John 8:44, and Luke 10:18

> "
> He did not foresee that attacking the Creator would be an attack upon creation and an attack upon the very laws that enable, uphold, sustain, govern, and promote everything created, including his very existence.
> "

C. **Thus, God's law of love & rest had already been impeached and His character questioned before this world was created.**
   1. Therefore, even though man was created free from sin, without the knowledge of evil, or propensity to sin, his loyalty - faith, love, and obedience to God - must be tested. Gen 1:26-31, 2:16, 17

II. **Mankind's failure of The Test of Loyalty** Gen 2:9, 15-17, 3:1-7
   A. What was the blossom and fruitage of mankind's disloyalty?
      1. Satan usurped man's loyalty from God to himself so that man's nature became bent towards evil, the blossom and fruitage of sin. There is now a law of sin in our natural born nature through heredity, which inclines us toward the evil clamors of our flesh, and works through our senses to war against the Spirit of God. What is the only remedy for our healing?
      We must "walk in the Spirit." Rom 7:18-25, Rom 8:1, 2, 12-14 Ga 5:16-18, 1 Cor 2:12-14, John 3:14-17, John 1:29, Num 21:5-9
      2. Mankind's spiritual nature died instantaneously, dethroning the Spirit of God from the temple of our being, and selfishness took the place of love. What must be our experience if we are to be recovered from this state of being? We must be born again, spiritually regenerated! Gen 3:7, 8, John 3:3,5-7, 1 Cor 2:12-14, 3:16, Rom 8:1-9, 12-14, 1 John 4:7, 8
      3. God made man to know only that which is good and consistent with His mind, character, and personality. Since the Fall, all that mankind thinks, does, devises, and produces is bent towards the mixing, the melding, the blending, the fusion of good with evil in a world that ever seeks to excuse, justify, normalize, and minimize evil, fulfilling the words of Satan that we "shall be as gods, knowing good and evil" (Gen 3:5). Is it possible to love this world and the things in it and love God at the same time? (1 John 2:15-17, John 15:18, 19, 17:15, 16, John 18:36)
      4. Thus sin with all its train of evil, unrest, rebellion, and death entered this our world, and God's seal of Rest was broken. Rom 5:12, Isaiah 59:1, 2, Heb 4:1, 2, 9-11
   B. **What is the hope for the human family?**
      1. God revealed His plan of human redemption. **The hope is God seeking after man!** Gen 3:8-15, Luke 19:10, John 3:16-21

2. The Lord put an enmity, a sense of hostility, in man towards Satan, thus preserving our free moral agency and enabling us to choose to turn from Satan's will to God's will (Gen 3:15, James 4:7-10, Heb 12:1-4, Rom 12:1, 2).

III. **Two Opposing Groups** - the woman versus the serpent, and the seed of the woman versus the Seed of the serpent. There would be active opposition and hostility between the followers of Christ and Satan, and between Christ and the followers of Satan, in the great controversy between Christ and Satan. Gen 3:14, 15
   A. The seed of the serpent are the followers of that old serpent called the Devil and Satan, who deceived the whole world. Rev 12:9
   B. The seed of the woman, which represents the pure Church, is Christ. Gen 3:15; Rev 12:1, 2, 5-10, Gal 3:16
   C. Early in human history these two opposing groups of people were developed.
      1. Cain walked in the footsteps of his father, the devil, who was a liar and murderer from the beginning. John 8:44, 1 John 3:12, Gen 4:5-10
      2. Abel walked in the footsteps of his Father, in the way of the cross, and became identified with his Father, the Lamb of God, slain from the foundation of the world. Gen 4:4, 8, Heb 11:4, Luke 9:23, 24, Rev 13:8
      3. Cain's descendants walked in the footsteps of their father and loved this world so much that every thought and imagination of their hearts was only evil continually.
      Humanism was their religion. Gen 4:16-24
         a. They went out from the presence of the Lord.
         b. They began the building of cities instead of scattering over the earth to replenish it as God commanded them.
         c. They gloried in the works of their own hands in forgetfulness of God.
         d. Lamech, 6th from Cain, introduced polygamy and continued in murder.
      4. Adam's posterity through Seth are reckoned as being the descendants of God their Father. Gen 5. In this righteous line was seen:
         a. Longevity of life.

       b. Enoch, the 7th from Adam, who walked so closely with God that the Scriptures say "He was not, for God took him". He was translated without seeing death and taken to Heaven.
Gen 5:24, Heb 11:5
As a preacher of righteousness, he taught about the judgment of the Flood - for he named his son Methuselah, which means "when he dies it shall come." He also preached about the 2nd Advent of Christ. Enoch was translated before his great grandson Noah was born. Gen 5:21-29, Jude 14, 15
      c. Noah, a preacher of righteousness, warned that rebellious generation of the coming flood, and built the Ark as a witness to them for the saving of all who would enter its sanctuary. Gen 6:8-22, Heb 11:7
D. The sons of God intermarry with the daughters of men: Seth's descendants marry the descendants of Cain, the righteous intermarry with the wicked and call forth the judgment of God.
    1. God, from the very beginning of sin in this world, had put enmity between the righteous and the wicked (Gen 3:15, 6:1-18).

Paul makes the contrast clear:
"Be ye not unequally yoked together with unbelievers: For what fellowship hath righteousness with unrighteousness? And what communion hath light with darkness? And what concord hath Christ with Belial (chief of devils)? Or what part hath he that believeth with an infidel? And what agreement hath the temple of God with idols? For ye are the temple of the living God; as God hath said, I will dwell in them, and walk in them; and I will be their God, and they shall be My people. Wherefore come out from them, and be ye separate, saith the Lord, and touch not the unclean; and I will receive you, and will be a Father unto you, and ye shall be My sons and daughters, saith the Lord Almighty." 2Cor 6:14-18

LEST THE WORLD BE OVERRUN BY THE ABOUNDING WICKEDNESS, THOSE STUBBORN REJECTORS OF GOD'S MERCIFUL PLEADINGS WERE SWEPT AWAY IN THE GREAT DELUGE CALLED THE FLOOD! GEN 7:11-24

Chapter IV

THE GREAT CONTROVERSY THE SEED OF THE SERPENT

I. **A New Beginning - After the Flood**
   A. By the 8 members of the family of Noah saved from the flood, the earth was to be repopulated. They were to disperse over the earth and replenish and subdue it. Gen 9:1-7, 18, 19
   B. In one of Noah's sons, Ham, was seen the same impiety and vileness of character that existed before the flood, though not grown to maturity.
      1. Ham's act of filial irreverence called forth a curse upon his posterity, the descendants of Canaan. Ham begot Cush, Mizraim, Phut, and Canaan. Gen 9:20-27
      2. Why curse Canaan? Ham had 4 children. It was because Canaan's posterity descended to the most degrading forms of heathenism in the worship of false gods. Though this prophetic curse had doomed them to slavery, the doom was withheld for centuries. God bore long with their impiety and corruption until they passed the limits of divine forbearance. What was the curse? They would be dispossessed and become bondmen to the descendants of Shem and Japheth. Geneses 9:25-27, PP, page 118

II. **When Sin Seeks to Perpetuate Itself - Enter Paganism**
   Seeing with what ease he could turn a people (the descendants of Cain) to glory in the works of their own hands in forgetfulness of God, Satan now sought to develop a religious system to war against the religion of Christ: Paganism, which is Spiritualism in its infancy.

THE GREAT CONTROVERSY THE SEED OF THE SERPENT

A. Historians have traced the beginning of Paganism, the worship of false gods, after the flood to Cush. AntiChrist (AC) 666, page 10
   1. Cush begot Nimrod whom the Scriptures say was a mighty hunter before/against/ in place of God. Gen 10:6, 8, 9, AC 666 page 35. Nimrod contended with God for the worship of the inhabitants of that ancient world. Complete Works of Flavius Josephus page 30, New Age & the Illuminati (NAI) page 17, 18.
   2. Instead of dispersing over the earth to replenish it as God commanded, Nimrod became the first king to unite the inhabitants of the earth into cities. Gen 10:8-10
   Here was the first attempt to establish a new world order.
B. The greatest exhibition of Nimrod's defiance of the living God recorded in Scriptures was the building of Babylon and the Tower of Babel. Gen 10:8-10, 11:1-9
   1. To make their city the metropolis of a universal empire whose glory would command the admiration of the world.
   2. To be a monument to humanism. PP, pg. 118
   3. To secure their own safety in case of another deluge, demonstrating their distrust of God, they intended to build the structure higher the height that was reached by the Flood. Patriarch & Prophets (PP) page 119
C. Nimrod and his descendants became the great instruments of Satan in promoting a counterfeit system of religion of the religion of Christ.
   1. **Paganism, based in the pseudo science of astrology, called the wisdom of the Chaldeans (Babylonians).** AC 666 page 68
   2. In all pagan philosophies **the doctrine of immortality of the soul is the foundation and center of their whole belief and worship.** Satan was the first to spawn this lie in the Garden of Eden when he told Eve "Ye shall not surely die" in direct opposition to the plain utterance of Jehovah that " In the day that ye eat thereof, ye shalt surely die." Gen 3:4, 2:16, 17

   > "
   > In all pagan philosophies the doctrine of immortality of the soul is the foundation and center of their whole belief and worship.
   > "

      a. This same lie used from Adam's time to our is the foundation of the falsehood of immortality of the soul, the basis of spiritualism, reincarnation, black magic, necromancy, purgatory, and all other mystic practices of the occults.

> **The whole system of the Mystery of Iniquity is based on this lie of the devil, of life after death.** NAI pg 29

D. Nimrod, also known by the deified name of Ninus among the early Assyrians, was said to have been killed, according to inscriptions, but his spirit became immortal and flew up to the sun and became Beelsaman, "Lord of Heaven" Two Babylons page 165, 264, NAI pg 30 Pagans believed that when they died, they too, like Nimrod, became immortal. They believed that the spirit living inside them is a divine spark that, at death, left the body and ascended to heaven and took possession of the stars. AC 66 6 page 68

E. After his death, Nimrod's wife, Semiramis, claimed that her womb was miraculously impregnated by a sunbeam, and that the child that she brought forth was the son of the sun god. She called his name Tammuz. **These three were the first pagan trinity: Nimrod, the sun god, the lord of heaven; Semiramis, the moon goddess, the queen of heaven; and Tammuz, the bright and morning star, the counterfeit messiah.** AC 666 page 28, 29

F. From the confounding of the languages and the scattering of the pagans at the Tower of Babel, this satanic system of religion, so firmly established in Babylon, overspread the world and has been used by the arch deceiver to war against the Seed of the woman from that time forward to the end of human history. Some of the nations to which this counterfeit religion of sun worship has spread as traced by archaeological findings are:

Nation	**Sun God**	**Mother God**	**Pagan Messiah**
Israel	Baal	Ashtoreth	Tammuz
Phoenicia	El	Astarte	Bacchus
Babylon	Bel Marduk	Rhea/Ishtar	Tammus
Assyria	Ninus/Shamash	Beltis/Ishtar	Hercules
Greece	Zeus	Aphrodite	Dionysus
Rome	Jupiter	Cybele/Diana	Attis
Egypt	Ra	Isis/Hathor	Osiris/Horus
India	Vishnu	Isi/Devaki	Krishna
China	P'an-ku	Heng-O/Ma-Tsoopo	Yi
Mexico	Teotl	Coatlicue	Quetzacoatl
Scandinavia	Odin	Frigg/Freyia	Balder

THE GREAT CONTROVERSY THE SEED OF THE SERPENT 25

    G. **Astrology is the pseudo science behind paganism** and it embraces the entire realm of the occult - witchcraft, sorcery, magic, hypnotism, fortune telling, etc. Its author is Satan who was Lucifer - the shining one, the illuminated one. And his spirit guides are the fallen angels, become demons. The chief star gods of the pagans are the gods of astrology which are believed to be just emanations of the one god, the sun god, the ruler of the zodiac. The origin of the number 666 is derived from astrology. Astrology uses the number 36 to divide the stars, and, if you add the numbers 1 through 36, you get 666. No ancient or modern day witch can cast a spell, no sorcerer perform an enchantment, no fortune teller predict the future without the aid of astrology. AC 666 page 68, 69

III. **The signs and symbols of paganism**. How far reaching and encompassing have the tentacles of this octopus of evil and iniquity reached?
    A. Paganism's signs and symbols have been used by our federal government since the founding of this great nation. They have been used as designs on the dollar bill, are plastered all over our federal buildings, are standing tall in Washington DC and in New York harbor, have been used by businesses as insignias on their products, and by the mass media as symbols of their organizations. They also form the Steeples and pinnacles on churches and have been used as symbols of Christianity (NAI 231-234)
    B. What are these signs & symbols so readily employed by government, businesses, the media, and churches alike?
        1. Phallicism, the veneration and worship of the male and female sex organs: Their union was symbolized in witchcraft as a point within a circle, and as two triangles uniting to make a hexagram. Here we find the origin of the wedding band where the finger represents the male sex organ and the ring the females.
           The obelisk on monuments, such as those in Washington DC and St Peters Square in the Vatican, and forming steeples on churches, are symbols of the phallus today known as the obelisk (NAI 45-50, 143-145).
        2. The all seeing eye at the top of a pyramid, representing the eye of Lucifer in witchcraft, is used as the symbol for CBS. The sun disk is used by ABC, and the peacock, a symbol of the sun god in China, India, and Japan, is used by NBC Television Networks.

3. Beneath a pyramid topped by the all-seeing eye on the back of the United States dollar bill is, **"Novus Ordo Seclorum" which means "New World Order"** (NAI 70-73, 222, 231-233).
4. The upside down cross with its cross bar broken down signifies, in modern day witchcraft, a rejection of Christianity by former Christians initiated into its rank. It is now use by Christians as a supposed symbol of peace.
5. The rainbow sign indicates to New Agers and the worshipers of Lucifer that Luciferians are building a bridge between man and the oversoul Lucifer. NAI page 222
6. The most evil sign in witchcraft, the hexagram, is formed by 13 pentagrams (the symbol for white & black magic) on the back of the dollar bill and as symbols on federal buildings.
7. The queen of heaven, the mother goddess, stands tall in New York Harbor, a gift from France, the only modern day nation which stands on record as having decreed by its legislative assembly that there was no God, and instituted the goddess of reason in His place.

IV. Regarding the feast and celebrations of paganism - how entrenched is our world in celebrating pagan holy days?
   A. The shortest day of the year, called by astronomers the winter solstice, is to the pagan sun worshipers the day the sun god is reborn. And the nativity of the sun, which fell on December 25th, was called by pagan Anglo Saxons, Yule-Day or Child's Day (AC 666 page 26,27, 31, 32)
   B. One of the strict observances a follower had to keep in the worship of Baal on pain of death if not done was to give honor to and recognize the sun god as the creator and lord of heaven. The day was kept holy and the people were commanded by law not to do any servile work. On this day the pagans would face the east to worship the rising sun. This day, called the Sun-day occurred the 1st day of each week. We notice that ancient Babylon had a Sun-day Law with a death decree. By the principle of the first and the last mention, this gives certainty to the fact that the last Babylon, Spiritual Babylon, will also have a Sun-day Law. AC 666 page 44.
   C. The pagans celebrated a New Year Festival known as Holy Week, the time of the resurrection of the dead vegetation god, Tammuz, who die in the Autumn and came back to life in the Spring. This was the time

when the pagan trinity appeared together in the heavens. The Sun-day of this Holy Week was the holy of holies to the pagans and was called Easter. This is Chaldean and means Astarte, one of the titles of Beltis, the queen of heaven in Nineveh. The queen of heaven was also the goddess of fertility. Because the hen and the rabbit were known for their many offspring they were her symbols. AC 666 page 103-112

V. **By Satanic Design - The Ultimate Objective of the Development of Spiritualism!**
   A. Satan has long been preparing for his final effort to deceive the world. The foundation of his work was laid by the assurance given to Eve in Eden: "Ye shall not surely die, for in the day that ye eat thereof then your eyes shall be opened, and ye shall be as gods, knowing good and evil." Gen 3:4, 5 GC page 561
   B. **Little by little Satan has prepared the way for his masterpiece of deception in the development of spiritualism.** He has not yet reached the full accomplishment of his designs, but it will be reached in the last remnant of time, the time of trouble. Says the prophet:
   "I saw three unclean spirits like frogs come out of the mouth of the dragon, and ....the beast, and ......the false prophet. For they are the spirits of devils, working miracles, which go forth unto the kings of the earth and of the whole world, to gather them to the battle of the great day of God Almighty." Rev 16 :13, 14, GC page 560-562
   As the crowning act in the great drama of deception, Satan himself will personate Christ......... In different parts of the earth, Satan will manifest himself among men **as a majestic being of dazzling brightness,** resembling the description of the Son of God given by John in Rev 1:13-15. Satan is not permitted to counterfeit the manner of Christ's Advent, but only those who have been diligent students of the truth will be shielded from this powerful delusion that takes the world captive. **How is it with you? Are you so firmly established upon God's Word that you will not yield to the evidence of your senses?** GC page 562, 624
   C. Did God anciently warn His follower about this counterfeit system of religion?
      1. In Deut 18:9-20 God points Israel away from this counterfeit with its false teachings and messiah to the true Messiah as they were coming out of Egyptian bondage to possess the Earthly Canaan.

2. In Jeremiah 10:2-5 God admonishes His people to "learn not the ways of the heathen (pagan), and be not dismayed at the signs of the heavens (astrology), for the heathen are dismayed at them, for the customs of the people are vain."
Why? See Jeremiah 10:10-15

Chapter V

THE GREAT CONTROVERSY THE SEED OF THE WOMAN

I. The Counterfeit, Paganism
   A. Satan had men worshiping the sun, the moon, the stars; graven images of men, animals, trees, insects, frogs, and rocks. The pagans worship everything except the Creator who created these things. NAI page 104, Rom 1:18-32
   B. Why did Satan invent Paganism?
      1. **To counterfeit the pure teachings of the gospel and hide his falsehood under the cloak of Christianity.**
         a. As in the true faith, paganism has its promised messiah, a form of baptism, a spiritual rebirth, a confession of sins, a communion, and the promise of immortality. NAI page 9
      2. Before the birth of the real incarnate of God, the Seed that should bruise the serpents head, the real Bright and Morning Star, Satan's messiah had already been preached and worshiped throughout the world, counterfeiting the religious rites passed down by the Patriarchs. Satan tried to destroy faith in the true faith by false gods, and when the written Word was given, he hoped the learned men of the world would look upon Christ as just another pagan messiah. Thus is the teaching of the New Age movememt. NA 666 pg 106
      3. In the ancient world Satan deceived millions with the darkness of pagan sun worship. In these modern days he has taken on a

brighter look, cloaking his pagan sun worship in the garments of Christianity, and coming in the name of Jesus. NAI page 197

II. **The seed of the Woman, From the Flood to Egypt.**
   A. The followers of Christ who preserved the knowledge of the True and Living God are recorded in Gen 11:10-27 from Shem to Abraham.
      1. So widespread and influential was Satan's counterfeit religion that overspread the earth from the scattering at the Tower of Babel that the records say that **Abraham was called out of Ur of the Chaldeans, out of Babylon, away from his kindred that served other gods.** Genesis 12:1-3, 15:7, 5, 6, 13-18 Joshua 24:2, 3, PP page 125, 126, 147
         a. **Called into a covenant relationship with God** who would make of him a great nation. Genesis 12:1, 2, 15:5, 6
         b. **Called to be the channel through whom all families of the earth would be blessed.** Genesis 12:1-3
         c. **Called to be perfect, and the father of the faithful.** Genesis17:1-5
         d. **Called to inherit and posses the land of promise, the Earthly Canaan.** Genesis 9:25-27, 17:8
         e. **Called to be the one through whom the promised Messiah would come.** Genesis 22:15-18
      2. Abraham was said to be the friend of God, God Himself bearing witness to his faithfulness, his fidelity, his integrity and his obedience. Genesis 18:17-19, 22:16-18, Isa 41:8
   B. The Patriarchs Isaac and Israel were the seed of Abraham who received the covenant blessing that God promised Abraham. Genesis 17:21, 26:1-5, 28:10-14, 32:24-28, 35:10-12, PP page 141
      1. The Patriarchal system of government in which the father was both priest and ruler proved to be successful in preserving the knowledge and worship of Jehovah from Shem to Abraham, and from Abraham to Israel and his 12 sons.
      2. Joseph, the 1st born son of Israel's beloved Rachel and favored of all his sons, was sold into bondage of Egypt in his youth. Troubled, but not distressed, perplexed, but not in despair, persecuted, but not forsaken, cast down, but not destroyed, Joseph resolutely fixed his affections, his faith, his loyalty upon the God of his father and was enabled to rise above his circumstances. And God blessed and

prospered him in all that he did, and endowed him with the gift of disclosing and interpreting dreams, thus preparing the way for him to be lifted out of his enslavement and his imprisonment to be God's agent in Egypt, a sovereign power at that time, 2nd in power only to Pharaoh, for the salvation not only of literal Israel, but of the world around them. This experience of Joseph was a typology of the Christian experience. Joseph was a type of Christ, Egypt a type of the world, and Israel a type of the Christian. The mighty deliverance and preservation of Egypt through 7 years of a dreadful famine should have bound the hearts of the Egyptians and surrounding nations in gratitude to Joseph and Joseph's God who foretold of the famine before it came to pass, and gave the remedy for it. 2 Cor 4:8-10 Psalms 105:17-23

3. With the 12 sons of Israel a core group was established out of which God would raise up a nation. PP page 232, Ex 1:7

   a. In God's providence the 12 sons of Israel and their families were brought down to Egypt and given land apart from the Egyptians. The antipathy they must encounter there on account of their occupation would enable them to remain a distinct and separate people and would serve to shut them out from participation in the idolatry of Egypt. There, God would multiply them and make of them a great nation. Genesis 15:5, 13, 14, Ex 1:7, Psalms 105:23-25, PP page 632

III. A Chosen People, From Egypt to Mt Sinai

A. As God began to deliver Israel out of Egyptian bondage, He made known to the Egyptians and all the surrounding nations that He was the only true and living God, the Creator of the heavens and the earth. Ex 7:1-7, Psalms 105:26-38, 106:7-23

   1. His power and glory was manifest to uproot from the heart of pagans the worship of the sun, moon, cattle, and other objects of creation they deified or made into graven images. Ex 7-13

   2. Not only to dispel the darkness of paganism did God mightily deliver Israel from bondage, but He purposed to strengthen Israel's faith, and reveal to them His loving watch-care, protection, and faithfulness as a covenant keeping God! Genesis 15:1-18, Deut 4:32-40, Deut 7:6-11

B. **At Sinai Israel was made an extension of the government of Heaven upon the earth, and was inducted into the church of Heaven with Jehovah as their God and King**. Ex 19:1-6 The government of Israel was administered in the name and by the authority of God. The work of Moses, the 70 elders, the rulers, and judges was simply to enforce the laws that God had given; they had no authority to legislate for the nation. Foreseeing that Israel would desire a king, God did not consent to a change in the principles upon which the nation was founded. The king was to be the vicegerent of the Most High God who was to be recognized as the Head of the nation, and His law was to be enforced as the supreme law of the land. PP 603

From Sinai to the possessing of the promised land God sought to set before Israel the great destiny and ideal that was theirs, and to preserve them from the evils of the pagans whom He would drive out before them. Deut 17:14-20

1. **He instructed them in statutes and judgments, and His 10 Commandment Law, the obedience of which would be their wisdom and understanding in the sight of the nations.** Deut 4:1-13, Ex 20:1-21
2. He warned them not to make a graven image of any figure of male/female of fish, beast, or human; nor of the sun, moon, stars, or any of the host of heaven, to worship or serve them. Deut 4:14-31
3. God instructed Israel to learn not the abominations of those nations who caused their children to pass through the fire, who used divination, observed times, and were enchanters, witches, charmers (hypnotist), consulter of evil spirits, and necromancers. Deut 18:9-15
4. **God purposed to set Israel on high, above all the nations of the earth, to be the head and not the tail, to be above only and not beneath, to make all people of the earth afraid of Israel.** Deut 7:1-11, 28;1-13
5. To bless Israel above all people and to take from Israel all the sickness and diseases that afflicted the pagans. Deut 7:14, 15

IV. A Chosen People - From Mt Sinai to Babylon
A. But sad is the Bible Commentary about God's chosen people. Time and time again, they fell before Satan's counterfeit pagan religion. Judges 2:6-15

1. As Israel was entering upon the promise land to posses it, the record states that after the death of Joshua, all the elders that outlived Joshua, and the generation who had seen the great works of the Lord, there rose up a generation that knew not the Lord and served Baal, the pagan lord of heaven, and Ashtaroth, the pagan queen of heaven. Judges 2:6-15
2. **When God allowed the enemies of Israel to take them captive**, they would cry unto the Lord and **He would raise up judges to deliver them.** But, with the death of the judge, the next generation would forsake the Lord and would worship and serve Satan's counterfeit trinity (Judges 2:16-23; 3:7-11, **Othniel;** Judges 4-5:1, **Deborah & Barak;** Judges 6 - 8, **Gideon**; Judges 11 & 12, **Jephthah**; Judges 13:1-5; 14-17:30, **Samson**).
3. After Samson's death we entered the days when "every man did what was right in his own eyes" (Judges 17:6, 21:25) until Eli judged Israel 40 years. However, when Eli failed to restrain his sons who made themselves vile, God's judgment brought his house to an end, and Samuel, God's anointed prophet, became the judge of Israel. Although Samuel judged Israel faithfully, his sons did not walk in his ways. In his old age, when he made them judges they "turned aside after lucre, and took bribes, and perverted judgment. Then the elders of Israel demanded of Samuel a king instead of his sons to judge them. (1 Sam 3:11-14, 19- 4:2, 11, 16-22, 8:1-8 Deut 17:14-20)
4. **Desiring to be like the surrounding nations, Israel added to their sins by rejecting Jehovah as their King, preferring an earthly, human monarch to go before them.** 1 Sam 8:7-20
5. God chose Saul according to the pride of heart that prompted the elders to demand a king: "Of noble and dignified bearing, in the prime of life, comely and tall, he appeared like one born to command." (1 Sam 9:2, 20, 21, 10:1, 17-25, 16:7). But "Saul was destitute of those higher qualities that constitute true wisdom," as time would show. Disobeying God's instruction given by Samuel on what to do in his first encounter with the Philistines, and not waiting for Samuel to come to offer burnt offering and sacrifices, Saul showed himself unfit to be the vicegerent of God" and was told that his kingdom would not continue. Nevertheless, the LORD

God affirmed His anointing of Saul as king and then instructed him to go and utterly destroy the Amalekites and all that they possess. However, instead of obeying the LORD, Saul preserved king Agag alive and spared the best of the sheep and all the animals that were good. Therefore, the LORD rejected him as king . "And Samuel said, **Hath the Lord as great delight in burnt offerings and sacrifices as in obeying the voice of the Lord? Behold, to obey is better than to sacrifice, and to harken then the fat of rams. For rebellion is as the sin of witchcraft, and stubbornness is as iniquity and idolatry. Because thou has rejected the word of the Lord, He has also rejected thee from being king."** And the kingdom was rent from him that day and Samuel was sent to anoint David as chosen of God to be His vicegerent. Saul subsequently had the priest of Nob slain. Having despised the counsel of Samuel when he was alive and slain the priest of God, Saul cut off all channels of communication with God. In his final battle with the Phillistines, Saul, in his desperation turned to a witch to have her bring Samuel up from the dead. Thus, Saul gave evidence of being completely possessed by Satan and of trusting in the lie of the devil - the immortality of the soul (1 Sam 10:5-8; 12:14, 15; 13:1-14; 1 Sam 15:1-23; 16:1, 7-14; 28:3-25

6. David became God's appointed vicegerent to rule His people Israel as king. His throne God would establish forever.
As a man after God's own heart, David's faith, love, and fidelity to God were a model for future kings. He showed his unflinching faith, fearlessness, and trust in God when Saul repeatedly hunted him down. Yet, when Saul fell into his hands, David honored him as the LORD'S anointed and would not allow his men to harm or slay him. **David also magnified humility of heart and repentance of soul when sin was found in him** (1 Sam 16:1, 12-13; 17:21-26; 1 Sam 17:32-37, 45-47; 24:9-12; 1 Kings 9:1-5; 11:31, 38; 15:1-5, 11; 2 Kings 12:1, 2; 16:1-3; 2 Kings 18:1-3; 22:1, 2; 2 Sam 12:1-24; Psalms 51)

7. **Solomon was Israel's wisest king. God appeared unto him in a dream and ask what He should give him.** Extolling God for His kindness towards David, His faithful servant, in giving him a son to sit upon his throne, **Solomon presented himself as a little child knowing not how to go out or come in, or how to**

govern so great a people. Then he **asked God to give him an understanding heart to judge His people.** So pleased was God with Solomon's humble request, He not only gave him wisdom, but riches and honor greater than any man before or after him. **Yet, Solomon had an affinity for beautiful women, women of every hew, shape, and taste, even women expressly forbidden by God to marry.** In addition **God forbade the king to multiply wives to himself.** Solomon's wisdom did not prevent him from disobeying God's will and it proved a snare to him in his old age, leading him into the abominable sins of participating in immoral rites and sacrificing children unto many of the gods of his 700 pagan wives. AC 666 pge 45, 1 Kings 3:6-14, 1Kings 11:1-8

    a. **So deeply laid was Solomon's sin that even though he himself repented and returned to the worship of Jehovah, the nation of Israel never fully recovered from sun worship.** The Lord declared that He would surely rend the kingdom so that only the tribes of Judah and Benjamin would cleave unto the posterity of King David. 1 King 11:9-13, 28-40

8. God gave 10 tribes to Jeroboam, "a mighty man of valor," whom Solomon saw as industrious and made him ruler over all the charge of the house of Joseph. When Solomon heard that God purposed to give Jeroboam 10 tribes, he sought to kill him, and Jeroboam fled into Egypt. 1 Kings 11:28-40

9. When Jeroboam and all Israel sought for reforms from Rehoboam after Solomons death, and he promised to make their yoke more grievous, the 10 tribes of Israel rebelled and made Jeroboam king of Israel. 1 Kings 12:1-5, 12-20 Jeroboam should have been grateful to God for making him king. However, he allowed his fear that the heart of Israel would return to Rehoboam, king of Judah, because Jerusalem was the center of worship. "Whereupon the king took counsel, and made 2 calves of gold, and said unto them, ... behold your god, O Israel, which brought thee up out of Egypt" (1 Kings 12;27-29). "And this thing became a sin" (1 Kings 12:30). Because of Israel's sin and rebellion, God used Shalmaneser, king of Assyria, as His instrument, to bring judgment upon Israel, to remove them from before His face as nation (1 King 13:31-14:20; 15:25-16:26; 2 Kings 17).

10. In the line of the kings of Israel after the kingdom was rent came Ahab, who walked in the sins of the kings before him and went so far as to marry Jezebel, the daughter of Ethbaal, King of the Zidonians. Together, they led Israel to serve and worship Baal. The Israelites were so degraded and blinded by Satan's counterfeit that they did not know whether Jehovah was Lord and Creator or Baal; or whether the prophets of Baal or the mighty Elijah was the genuine prophet of God (AC 666, page 71; 1 Kings 16:29-22:39). The contest on Mt Carmel decided the issue and the people returned to the worship of Jehovah. 1 Kings 18:19-40

The message that Elijah gave to Israel is the same message to be given to the Christian world today **How long halt ye between two opinions? "If the LORD be God, follow Him, but if Baal, then follow him."** (1 Kings 18:21). It is a message calling a people to the pure unadulterated gospel of Jesus, unmingled with pagan customs, rites, traditions, symbols, and festivities (Mal 4:4-6)

> "
> The message that Elijah gave to Israel is the same message to be given to the Christian world today "How long halt ye between two opinions? "If the LORD be God, follow Him, but if Baal, then follow him.
> "

In spite of this reprieve and acknowledgement that "the LORD He is God," Israel progressed in her sin and rebellion against the Lord in worshiping Satan's counterfeit gods until God allowed the Assyrians to scatter her and take her captive, and remove her from before His face as a nation upon the face of the earth during reign of Hoshea. 2King 17

11. Ahaz reigned in Judah at the time of Israel's removal and did evil. **Hezekiah,** his son, followed him and **did what was right in the sight of the Lord, and trusted in God like no other king before or after him.** 2 King 18:1-12, 2 Chron 31:20, 21 Yet, when given opportunity to reveal God to the Babylonians, who came to Jerusalem to learn of the God who could turn their god back 10 degrees as a sign of His healing the king of Judah, Hezekiah forgot God and boasted in his treasures and wealth. This brought the judgment of God that all the treasures of the palace in Jerusalem would be carried away into Babylon. Hezekiah repented & led Jerusalem in repentance, and prepared his heart to trust and depend fully upon God before the Assyrian invasion of Judea. 2 Kings 20: 1-11, 12-19, 2 Chron 32: 24-31, 1-8

12. Hezekiah was followed by his son, **Manasseh,** who **led Judah into the bases and most abominable idolatry of all the kings of Judah and Israel.** 2 King 21:1-16, 2 Chron 33:3, 6, 7 Manasseh worshiped Baal and the host of heaven, made his son to pass through the fire, observed times, used enchantments, and dealt in familiar spirits and wizards. He slew the prophet Isaiah and all who would continue in the worship of Jehovah. Yet, when taken captive and thrust into prison, he repented and was converted. But the nation continued in idolatry and Satan's counterfeit sun worship. 2 Chron 33:11-16
13. Though Manasseh's grandson, Josiah, brought about a national reformation and revival in Judah, his 4 sons - Jehoahaz, Eliakim/Jehoiakim, Jehoiachin, and Mattaniah/Zedekiah - did that which was evil in the sight of the Lord, until the nation was carried away into Babylonian captivity. 2 Kings 23-25
It was during the reign of these last 4 kings of Judah that God revealed to Jeremiah and Ezekiel the depth of apostasy in the nation, and their worshiping of Satan's counterfeit triune gods.
The religious leaders were shown worshiping the sun god with their backs to the temple of Jehovah. Eze 8:15, 16 **The people made cakes (hot cross buns) to the queen of heaven** and poured out drink offerings unto her and other gods and burned incense unto her. Jer 44:15-18
The women were seen weeping for Tammuz - the lord of of death and rebirth, the vegetation god - in the spring during the pagan new year festival holy week, beginning with the Sun-day when Tammuz was supposedly resurrected from the dead and all vegetation sprung forth into newness of life.
This season of weeping for Tammuz is **known by modern day sun worshipers as Lent.** And the **Sunday of the holy week, called the holy of holies by the pagans, is known as Easter to both pagans and professed Christians alike** (Eze 8:7-16).
On this special Sun-day, the pagans would hold what modern Christians today call "sunrise services" (AC 666 pg 43, 44).
E. **Thus came the judgments of God upon a chosen people.**
1. **A people whom the Lord had purposed to make sovereigns of the earth.** Deut 7:6, 28:1-13

2. The vineyard of the Lord, **fenced and hedged in by His Holy Law, with the strong tower of the Earthly Sanctuary and the Levitical Priesthood to lighten the pathway before them to the throne of God and provide shelter from sin.** Isa 5:1-14
3. **And the sovereignty of the earth passed from the hands of a chosen people into the hands of others until He comes whose right it is.** Eze 21:24-27

F. From the carrying away of Judah and Jerusalem into Babylonian captivity, **into the hands of how many others would the sovereignty of the earth pass until He comes whose right it is?**
   1. This question propels us into a study of the prophecies of Daniel, beginning with chapter 2.

Chapter VI

DANIEL 2 - THE RISE AND FALL OF PAGAN UNIVERSAL EMPIRES

I. **Origin of Paganism, Satan's Counterfeit of the Religion of Christ.**
   A. After the flood, Nimrod and his descendants, the founders and builders of Babylon, were the instruments of Satan in promoting this counterfeit religion of **Paganism, based in pseudo science of astrology, and called the wisdom of the Chaldeans (Babylonians).** Gen 10:8-10, 11:1-9
   B. **The chief god of paganism is the sun god, the ruler of the zodiac.**
   C. **The principle doctrine of all pagan philosophies is the doctrine of immortality of the soul, the foundation and center of their whole belief system and worship.** Gen 2:17, 3:4, 5
   D. Babylonian mysticism, called illuminism, teaches that man is a microcosm, a miniature universe, and the ruler of nature, capable of spiritually expanding himself to become god.
   E. This astrological system of religion embraces all forms of the occult - witchcraft, sorcery, magic, spiritualism, hypnotism, fortune telling, soothsaying, and others. It's proponents profess to make known mysteries and hidden things entirely beyond human foresight and penetration by the aid of supernatural agencies - spiritual beings, evil spirits, spirits of the dead, and occult power of nature. Satan used this system to counterfeit and war against the religion of Christ.

II. **The sovereignty of the earth passes from the hands of a chosen people into the hands of others until He comes whose right it is.**
Eze 21:24-27
   A. **Israel, Judah and Jerusalem failed to allow God to exalt them to the position of sovereigns of the earth** by repeatedly falling before Satan's counterfeit system of sun worship. They bowed before Baal, the sun god, the creator and lord of heaven; Astaroth the queen of heaven, the mother of god; and Tammuz, the son of the sun god, the counterfeit messiah. Eze 8:5-16, Jer 7:17-31, 44:15-30
   B. Into the hands of how many pagan empires would the sovereignty of the earth pass "until he come whose right it is" (Ezek 21:27)?
   This question immediately propels us into a study of the prophecies of Daniel.

III. **Nebuchadnezzar, king and servant of the Most High God**
   A. Nebuchadnezzar, king of Babylon, a vigorous and brilliant commander, and physically as well as mentally a strong man, was ordained of God to become the greatest man of his time in all the near east as a soldier, statesman, and architect. DR
   B. **Babylon was chosen of the Lord as His servant to punish his rebellious people and subdue all nations.** Jer 25:9-12, 27:5-8, 11
   C. As Nebuchadnezzar was contemplating the future in 603BC and wondering what lay ahead, God gave the monarch a dream that startled and greatly troubled him, & then took the memory of the dream away while leaving a deep and lasting impression upon his mind. Dan 2:1-12, 29
   D. In God's providence, the king summoned the wise men, who were Babylonian nationals, of whom Daniel, Hananiah, Mishael, and Azariah were not reckoned. Dan 2:2, I Part E
      1. **The Lord cleaved Israel out to Himself to be His sovereign representatives in the earth.** Through them He purposed to reveal Himself as the only true and living God, and the Creator, who alone is worthy to be worshiped. When Israel failed to allow God to accomplish His purpose through them, they forfeited the sovereignty of the earth, and the LORD gave it into the hands of others, until He comes whose right it is. Now, He will accomplish in Israel's captivity what they failed to allow Him to accomplish in

DANIEL 2 - THE RISE AND FALL OF PAGAN UNIVERSAL EMPIRES 41

their freedom and sovereignty. And, He will do this through those who prove themselves faithful and true to Him. Dan 1:1, 3, 4, Deut 4:5-8, 33-40
   2. Were the wise men of Babylon able to reveal to king Nebuchadnezzar his dream? Dan 2:4-13, 27, 28
  E. The dream revealed to the servant of God. Dan 2:19-36
   1. Daniel described a metallic image of decreasing worth from the head to the toes, though not decreasing in strength. The material forming the body part of the image represents the kingdom, not the body part. Thus, division only occurs as indicated in the prophecy.

IV. **Babylon - 606 to 538 BC**
  A. **"Thou art this head of gold."** Dan 2:37, 38
   God foretells Babylons rise to glory.
   1. A golden cup in the Lord's hand. DR 33, Jer 51:7
   2. The glory of kingdoms, the beauty of the Chaldeans excellency. Isa 13:19
   3. The golden city. Isa 14:4
  B. Nebuchadnezzar reigned 45 years and died Aug-Sept 561 BC. The first 3 years he reigned as co-regent with his father, Nabopolassar. In the 1st year of the reign of Neriglisser 560 BC, the Medes revolted, and was joined by Persia. Neriglisser spent 3 years preparing for an inevitable war. In the 4th year a fierce battle ensued in which he was slain 556 BC. Cyaxares was king of Media, and Cambyses I, king of Persia. Cyrus, the son of Cambyses and nephew of Cyaxares (known as Darius the Mede), was commander of the allied forces. Between the death of Neriglisser and the 16th year of Nabonadius in 540 BC, Cyrus succeeded Cambyses to the throne of Persia, and, as general, led the allied powers in conquering all the tribes of Central Asia. In 540 BC, he was ready to make a descent upon mighty Babylon, the only city in all the east that held out against him. With preparations having been made in 540 BC, Cyrus marched towards Babylon in the spring of 539 BC, but was delayed a year. He launched his campaign and conquered it in the spring of 538 BC at the age of 61. (Jer 51:45, 46). Cyrus was named by the Lord over 100 years before his birth, and told what he would do 174 years before he did it. GEP pg 49-57

V. Medo-Persia 538 to 331 BC

A. The breast and the arms of silver represent the joint empire of the Medes and Persians.
B. Dan 5 reveals the fall of the last reigning king of Babylon to be Belshazzar. GEP Chp 3, Jer 27:7
C. God prophesied over 100 years before Cyrus' birth that He would raise him up as the LORD'S anointed servant (Isa 45:1).
D. Babylon was not taken by the power of human ingenuity or machination. No weapon then devised would have enabled the Medes & Persians to take the city of Babylon. **It was only by the providence and judgment of God that Babylon was taken.**
Isa 45:1-6, 51:1-9, 11-14, 25-32, 39, 40, 54-58, Dan 5:18-31
E. **The Persian Empire was used of God to restore His people to Jerusalem for the rebuilding of the temple and the city,** though subject to pagan powers. Ezra 6:14, Ezra 1:1-4 (Cyrus 536BC), Ezra 6:1-12 (Darius Hystaspes 520BC), 7:11-26, (Artaxerxes 457BC)
F. The battle of Arbela in 331BC marked the downfall of the Persian Empire.

VI. Greece, the Macedonian Empire 331 to 168 BC

A. The belly and thighs of brass corresponds to the 3rd kingdom that would arise to take the sovereignty of the earth - Greece, led by Alexander the Great. DR 42-44
B. The battle of Arbela, in 331 BC, was a deciding point in the contest between the Greeks and Persians. Though they were outnumbered 20 to 1, the Greeks won a decisive victory, and Alexander became absolute lord over the Persian Empire to an extent that had never been attained by any of its own kings.
C. The battle of Pydna in Macedonia marked the downfall of the Grecian Empire.

VII. Rome 168 BC to 476 AD

A. **"The arms of the republic, sometimes vanquished in battle, always victorious in war, advanced with rapid steps toward the Euphrates, the Danube, the Rhine, and the ocean: And the images of gold, or silver, or brass, that might serve to represent the nations and their kings, were successively broken by the iron monarchy Rome"** (Edward Gibbons, The Decline of the Roman Empire. vol III, Chp 38, page 64, DR 44-45

DANIEL 2 - THE RISE AND FALL OF PAGAN UNIVERSAL EMPIRES   43

B. Attacked by barbarians in the west and a nation propagating a new counterfeit religion in the east, Rome was broken up, but would continue to be a power to be reckoned with. Evidence of the continuing presence of Rome is given by the iron in the feet and toes.

VIII. **Period of the Divided Kingdoms DR 44-49**
   A. **The 10 nations most instrumental in the breakup of Western Rome,** and which, at some time in their history, held respective portions of Roman territory as separate and independent kingdoms were:

   1. Alemani   - Germany   6. Burgundians - Switzerland
   2. Franks   - France   7. Lombards   - Italy
   3. Visigoths   - Spain   8. Heruli
   4. Suevi   - Portugal   9. Ostrogoths
   5. Anglo Saxons   - Britain   10. Vandals

   The last three were plucked up by the Papacy.
   B. **Rome was the last of this world's universal empires.** After its breakup and the formation of the divided kingdoms - some strong as iron, others weak as clay - says the prophet "They shall mingle themselves together with the seed of men: But they shall not cleave one to another, even as iron is not mixed with clay" (Dan 2:43)
   C. **The rock cut out without hands** and smashing the image in the toes and utterly destroying the clay, the iron, the brass, the silver, and the gold **represents Christ setting up His everlasting kingdom,** the next and last universal earthly kingdom (Deut 32:41Pet 2:4-9, Dan 2:34, 35, 44-46).
   D. **All attempts to establish a universal empire between the breakup of Rome and the establishment of Christ's Kingdom are doomed to failure.** History bears witness to the fact in the attempts already made by: **Charlemagne, Charles V, Louis XIV, Napoleon, and Hitler.** And it will stand on record as witness against those who are even now attempting to establish a new one world order:
      1. **The international financial power brokers** who control nations monetary systems through such secret organizations as the Council on Foreign Relations, the Trilateral Commission in America, the Insti-

> ❝
> *All attempts to establish a universal empire between the breakup of Rome and the establishment of Christ's Kingdom are doomed to failure.*
> ❞

tute of International Affairs in England, and the international Bilderberg Group and the United Nations (NAI page 240-245).
   2. **New Age, Luciferian Conspirators** who promote a diabolical scheme to bring about a one world religion and one world government through the medium of the United Nations. NAI page 245-247
   3. **The Papacy** who promotes the ecumenical movement to unite all Christian churches into her fold, uniting through the 2 great errors that they hold in common - the immortality of the soul and Sunday sacredness which forms a bond of sympathy with Rome, Spiritual Babylon. AC 666 page 232-245 Working through its secret order of Jesuits, Rome has infiltrated every level of governments, banking institutions, universities, churches, medias, and businesses with the objective of bringing the world back under the control of Rome.
   All of whom promote the teaching of pagan Babylonian mysticism.

IX. **Behind the scene of human events, God is in control.**
   A. "In the history of the nations the student of God's word may behold the literal fulfillment of divine prophecy." PK 501-502
      1. "Babylon, shattered and broken at last, passed away because in prosperity its rulers regarded themselves as independent of God, and ascribed the glory of their kingdom to human achievement," making God their refuge only when harassed and perplexed.
      2. "The Medo-Persian realm was visited by the wrath of Heaven because in it God's law had been trampled underfoot."
      "Wickedness, blasphemy, and corruption prevailed among the people, and the fear of the Lord had found no place in the hearts of the vast majority."
      3. The kingdoms that followed were even more base and corrupt, and these sank lower and still lower in the scale of moral worth.
   B. **Prophecy has traced the rise and progress of the worlds greatest empires - Babylon, Medo-Persia, Greece, and Rome.**
   History has repeat itself. Each has had its period of test, each has failed, its glory faded, and its power departed (PK 535-537)
   In rejecting the principles of God, each nation has wrought its own ruin, yet a divine overruling purpose has manifestly been at work

throughout the ages. "The power exercised by every ruler on the earth is Heaven imparted; and upon his use of the power thus bestowed, his success depends. "To understand that "Righteousness exalted a nation," that "The throne is established by righteousness," and "upholden by mercy," to recognize the outworking of these principles in the manifestation of His power who "removeth kings and setteth up kings" this is to understand the true philosophy of history" (Prov 14:34, 16:12, 20:28; Dan 2:20, 21; PK 502)

Chapter VII

DANIEL 3 - SUN WORSHIP - THE IMAGE AND THE DEATH DECREE

I. In the Providence of God
   A. **Babylon, the riches of all earthly kingdoms, might have stood unchallenged as the agent of God** had her rulers kept before them the fear of Jehovah. God would have given them the wisdom and power that would have bound them to Him and kept them strong.
   But, as with many now living, prosperity was accompanied by a forgetfulness of God, a proud and self indulgent spirit that acted apart from and independent of God, and ascribed to human achievement the possession and glory thus secured (humanism in the highest degree). PK 501, Jer 51:9, 13, 24
      1. God, foreseeing this folly of the rulers of Babylon, prophesied its fall in the shadow of foretelling its rise to glory. Jer 25:9-12, 51:7-11, Isa 13:19-22, 14:4
   B. God knew the character of the man that would sit upon the throne of Babylon when He would use him to punish His rebellious people.
      1. Nebuchadnezzar, a man of such an impressionable character that, though pagan and ignorant of the living God, would humble himself and confess and acknowledge God before men & nations when his conscience was convinced through the evidence given him of the manifest power and glory of God.

DANIEL 3 - SUN WORSHIP - THE IMAGE AND THE DEATH DECREE

II. The Image of Daniel 2
A. **In the image of gold, silver, brass, iron, and clay, the Omniscient God revealed to Nebuchadnezzar human history from his time to when Christ would set up His everlasting kingdom and utterly destroy all earthly kingdoms.**
  1. Deeply impressed with the fear of the Lord, the king humbled himself before the God of Heaven. But as a result of his ambitious campaigns to subdue all nations with its attending prosperity and his desire to exalt himself, pride eventually eclipsed his acknowledgement of God, and he returned to his idol worship with increased zeal and bigotry.
  Dan 2:47-49, 3:28-30, PK 503-50

III. Truth Mixed with Error - The Image of Dan 3 and Rev 13 - The Principle of the 1st and the Last Mention - A Typology
A. Dan 3 opens with the statement "Nebuchadnezzar the king made an image of gold, …. and set it up in the plain of Dura, in the province of Babylon." Instead of reproducing the image like he had seen it, he made it all of gold from the head to the toes, signifying that Babylon was to be an eternal, indestructible, all powerful kingdom that would break in pieces all other kingdoms and stand forever.
  1. That which God had given as a revelation of His purposes for the nations was now being used to serve the purpose of the king, to glorify and exalt himself. An image no doubt in his own likeness, the highest representative of his god, the sun god, the ruler of the zodiac. To the Babylonian sun worshipers gold was considered the metal of the sun, condensed sunshine.
B. In Dan 3 we find the literal ruler of Babylon making an image to pagan sun worship, erecting it in the province of Babylon, in the plain of Dura. In Rev 13:11-14 we find the representative rulers of Spiritual Babylon making an image to spiritual pagan sun worship and erecting it in the province of the earth, in the plain of the United States of America.

IV. A Universal Decree - Civil Power Imposing a Religious Act - Obey or be killed.
A. In Dan 3 the literal ruler of Babylon summoned to appear before him on the plain of Dura all persons of importance, representatives of the people - princes, governors, captains, judges, counselors, treasurers,

sheriffs, and all rulers of the provinces - for the dedication of his image. **A universal decree was made to all peoples, nations, and languages thus represented,** that at the sound of all kinds of music, they were to bow down and worship the golden image or "be cast into the midst of a burning fiery furnace." Dan 3:3-6

B. In Rev 13:11-17, the representative agents of Spiritual Babylon are seen decreeing that all who dwell upon the earth shall worship the image of Spiritual Babylon (vs 1-3) by receiving her mark in their right hand or forehead, or they will be cast into a fiery furnace of affliction - that is, they will be forbidden to buy or sell, and they will finally be killed.

C. Gathered on the plain of Dura were rulers from Judah & Jerusalem as well as the 3 Hebrews who held positions of high honor in the court of king Nebuchadnezzar. At the sound of the music, these rulers, like the rulers of other nations, prostrated themselves before the golden image with their faces to the ground.

D. So shall it be when the decree goes forth at the end of time to worship the image of Spiritual Babylon. Many now professing to be Christians, Spiritual Israelites, will prostrate themselves and receive the mark or sign of allegiance to Satan's pagan sun religion when cloaked in the garments of Christianity and coming in the name of Christ.

V. **Accused & Maligned, But Faithful & Loyal in the Time of Trouble.**
   A. **Hannaniah, Mishael, and Azariah** were the only ones in all the host of that worshiping multitude that **proved themselves faithful and loyal to God at whatever cost to themselves.** The law of God forbade them bowing before an idol or worshiping false gods. Such homage they could render to God alone. Ex 20: 2-7
   B. **Nebuchadnezzar gave the Hebrews a second chance, and, in pompous pride, defied any God to deliver them out of his hands.** Also, as a display of his power he called for the mightiest men of his army to bind the Hebrews and cast them into the fiery furnace heated 7 times hotter than usual. Dan 3:14, 15
      1. Calmly facing the king, the Hebrews said If this is your decision, "our God whom we serve is able to deliver us ……. out of thine hand, O king." Their faith strengthened … and with triumphant assurance born of implicit trust in God, they added, "But if not, be it known unto thee, O king, that we will not serve thy gods, nor worship the golden image which thou has set up."

DANIEL 3 - SUN WORSHIP - THE IMAGE AND THE DEATH DECREE

>   God delivered His children in - and not from - the time of trouble of the burning fiery furnace of affliction.
>   PK 505-508, Dan 3:16-18
> C. In the experience of the followers of Christ in literal Babylon, we may read the experience of Spiritual Israel, the Christian Church, at the end of time. **The fidelity and implicit trust in God exhibited by the 3 Hebrews will be required of those living upon the earth when Spiritual Babylon shall seek to cast the followers of Christ into a fiery furnace of affliction.** 1Cor 10:11-13, Rom 15:4, Dan 12:1, Rev 13:11-17

VI. The True Principles of Religious Liberty

A. King Nebuchadnezzar exhibited a spirit contrary to the spirit of Christ. **"It is no part of Christ's mission to compel men to receive Him. It is Satan, and men actuated by his spirit, that seek to compel the conscience.** Under a pretense of zeal for righteousness, men who are confederate with evil angels bring suffering upon their fellow men, in order to convert them to their ideas of religion." **"There can be no more conclusive evidence that we possess the spirit of Satan than the disposition to hurt and destroy those who do not appreciate our work, or who act contrary to our ideas"** (DA, p 487)

> ❝ *"It is no part of Christ's mission to compel men to receive Him. It is Satan, and men actuated by his spirit, that seek to compel the conscience.* ❞

B. The Constitution of the United States guarantees liberty of conscience in the establishment clause - Amendment I. Those seeking to establish a new world order with a one world religion and one world government do not regard this principle. Insidiously they will promote common good consensus for the majority to undermine the individual's liberty of conscience with the ultimate objective of reducing the masses to a controllable herd in which independent thinking is marginalized.

C. Papal Rome, to whom Satan primarily and Pagan Rome secondarily gave his seat, power, and great authority stands on record as hating this principle of liberty of conscience. "The absurd and erroneous doctrines or ravings in defense of liberty of conscience are a most pestilential error - a pest of all others, most to be dreaded in a state." Pope Pius IX in his Encyclical Letter of August 15, 1854, GC 564

D. When Nebuchadnezzar was humbled to acknowledge the sovereignty of God, and show Him reverence by making a royal confession of allegiance as widespread as the Babylonian Realm, he did right. It was right for the king to make public confession, and to seek to exalt the God of Heaven above other gods: But in endeavoring to force his subjects to make a similar confession of faith and to show similar reverence, he exceeded his right as a temporal sovereign. **He had no more right, either civil or moral, to threaten men with death for not worshiping God, then to make a decree consigning to the flames all who refused to worship his golden image.** Dan 3:28-30, PK 510

E. **God never compels the obedience of man. He leaves all free to choose whom they will serve.** 1Kings 18:21, Josh 24:14, 15, Ezek 33:11, Deut 30:19, 20

Chapter VIII

DANIEL 7 PART 1 - THE ATTRIBUTES OF THE UNIVERSAL EMPIRES

I. **A Bible Principle At Work**
   A. By the principle of enlargement through repetition the Divine Teacher increases our knowledge and understanding.
   "For God speaketh once, yea twice, yet man perceiveth it not."
   Job 33:14
   1. Earlier prophecies lay the foundation for later prophecies.
      The details accumulate until like an artist dipping his brush in different colors, a complete picture is painted.
   2. Increasing light is shed upon the earlier prophecies revealing greater details, refining the information already given, and enlarging upon it.

II. **A Foundational Prophecy**
   A. **The vision of Dan 2 is a foundational prophecy upon which the series of visions that God gave to Daniel in Chapters 7-12 are based.**
   1. In the metallic image and the rock cut out without hands, God revealed human history in the political rise & fall of universal empires spanning a period of over 2600 years. As we studied into this prophecy and the interpretation thereof we learned that only 4 pagan empires would arise to take the sovereignty of the earth from the time of the carrying away of the Jews into Babylonian captivity to the 2nd Advent of our Lord: Babylon, Medo-Persia, Greece, & Rome. The prophecy admits, avows, acknowledges no

other. Therefore, any subsequent vision that introduces a kingdom, nation, or empire as universal, as taking the sovereignty of the earth in the same time frame must of necessity be Babylon, Medo-Persia, Greece, or Rome.

III. Prophetic Symbols Dan 7:1-3
A. **Four winds of strife are** used to portray scenes of war, revolution, political commotion, strife, and conquest as nations out of the north, the south, the east, and the west clash. Jer 25:31-33, 49:36, 37, GC page 439-440
B. **The great sea** in prophecy represents peoples, multitudes, nations, and tongues - Hence a land greatly inhabited. Rev 17:15
C. **Beast** represents universal kingdoms and empires. Dan 7:17, 23
D. **Horns** symbolize kingdoms, nations, powers. Dan 7:24
E. **Thus, the picture that is painted in Dan 7, is scenes of war, political commotion, revolution, and conquest by which nations have attained to power amid the teeming multitudes, nations, and peoples of the eastern hemisphere of the earth.**

IV. Beast of Prey - The Nature and Character of the Universal Empires
A. **The lion with eagles wings.** As the lion is king of beast, its roar and strength symbolizes the might of **the Babylonian kingdom under Nebuchadnezzar.** The eagles wings signifies the swiftness and rapidity of conquest with which he extended his empire. Jer 4:7, 13, 50:17, Habb 1:5-9, DR Chp 7
B. **The bear which arched itself up on one side, having three ribs in it's mouth, and receiving the command to arise, devour much flesh symbolizes the kingdom of Medo-Persia.** Jer 51: 11
   1. Like a bear, the Medes and Persians were cruel and rapacious, robbers, and spoilers of the people. DR chp 7
   2. The arching itself up on one side signified that one of the powers of this dual empire would have preeminence over the other.
   3. The command to devour and the 3 ribs refer to the stimulus given to the Medes and Persians to overthrow Babylon, and they especially oppressed the provinces of Babylon, Lydia, and Egypt.
C. **The leopard-like beast with the 4 heads and 4 wings of a fowl symbolize the 3rd kingdom that would arise** out of the warring nations of the earth - **Greece.** DR chp 7.

1. If 2 wings on the lion signified swiftness and rapidity of conquest, how much more does 4 wings on the leopard. The conquest by the Greeks under Alexander the Great had no parallel in ancient times for suddenness and rapidity.
2. The brevity of Alexander's brilliant career is implied by the 4 heads. At the height of his conquest, Alexander met with sudden death brought on by a fever resulting from a drunken debauch.

   His leading generals then warred amongst themselves and eventually divided the empire toward the north, the south, the east, and the west:
   a. **Lysimachus possessed** Thrace and parts of Asia on the Hellespont and the Bosphorus in **the north.**
   b. **Ptolemy possessed** Egypt, Lydia, Arabia Palestine, and Coele-Syria to **the south.**
   c. **Cassandra possessed** Macedonia and Greece to **the west.**
   d. **Seleucus possessed** Syria and all the rest of Alexander's dominion in **the east.**

D. **Inspiration finds no beast in nature to which hoofs, heads, horns, wings, teeth, or nails may be added to describe the 4th kingdom.** Hence it is nondescript. Though Dan 7 fails to name any of the 4 beast, in describing the 4th beast **we are plainly told that it is the fourth kingdom upon the earth, and that it is universal, for it shall devour the whole earth.** Our thoughts are immediately carried back to the vision of the metallic image and its forth kingdom and we look for similarities.
   1. **The nondescript beast is** said to be "dreadful and terrible, and strong exceedingly; and it had great iron teeth: it devoured and break in pieces, and stamp the residue with the feet of it: and it was diverse from all the beast that were before it; and it had 10 horns" (Dan 7:7, 23, 24)
   2. **The forth kingdom of the metallic image** is said to "be strong as iron: forasmuch as iron breaketh in pieces and subdueth all things: and as iron that breaketh all these shall it break in pieces and bruise" (Dan 2:40). The iron is seen to permeate into the feet and toes mixed with potters clay (Dan 2:41, 42)
   3. **How accurately the same kingdom is portrayed in both visions.** And since this kingdom is universal, we know from our

foundational prophetic study in Dan 2 that it can only be one of the 4 universal empires. Taking these factors together, **Rome is clearly the kingdom thus represented.** As soon as this fact is established, by virtue of the clear line of succession portrayed in the prophecy, the other 3 kingdoms stand up to identify themselves even as we have concluded above.

4. But the vision of the 4th beast goes further then the vision of the metallic image. A strange movement is portrayed to occur during the period of the divided kingdoms represented by "the feet and toes, part of potters clay, and part of iron" (Dan 2:41, 42), and by the 10 horns (Dan 7:24).

   There arises a little horn kingdom, initially smaller than the 10 horn kingdoms, but becoming, in time, more stout yet diverse from them. This little horn kingdom arises with the power and the authority of a political kingdom, for it plucks up, destroys, and roots out 3 of the original 10 kingdoms. Yet, it is seen to be religious in nature, character, and activity, for it wars against the saints of the Most High and thinks to change that law of the Most High which is set in time.

V. **Satanic Warfare Against God**
   A. **In Babylon we witness Satan's power to establish a counterfeit religion to the religion of Christ** - the worship of the sun god in place of the worship of the Son of God. This sun worship is based in the pseudo science of astrology, and, embracing the entire realm of the occult, is steeped in idolatry, the personification of all vileness.
   B. **In Medo-Persia we see a despotic power that trampled the law of God underfoot.** Through her Satan sought to exterminate the people of God (Esther).
   C. **In Greece** Satan worked through a power that gained no glory in either it's government or religion, but in the power of her intellect.

   > Here the wisdom and philosophical reasoning of the prince of evil was developed and went forth to permeate all of society, a mixture and fusion of good and evil

   Here the wisdom and philosophical reasoning of the prince of evil was developed and went forth to permeate all of society, a mixture and fusion of good and evil (Gen 3:4, 5).

D. **In Rome we see** a combination of the Satanic activity and characteristics of all the others:
   1. **The philosophical reasoning and wisdom of Greece.**
   2. **The tyrannical rule of Persia.**
   3. **The counterfeit system of religion of Babylon,** at first strictly pagan, afterward, a subtle and cunning instilling of paganism in the heart while Christianity is outwardly observed, a destruction working from within outward defacing the image of God in mind, in heart, and in the soul. **Pagan Rome was call the New Babylon; the Papacy is called Spiritual Babylon.**

Chapter IX

DANIEL 7 PART 2

THE PAPACY AND JUDGMENT, JUDGMENT, & JUDGMENT

I. Troubled, Perplexed, and Grieved in Spirit
   A. From the interpretation given of the beast of prey seen rising out of the sea tossed to and fro by the winds striving upon it, the prophet appears to have no difficulty.
      1. "These great beast, which are 4, are 4 kings which shall arise out of the earth." No doubt, the prophets mind carried him back to the vision of the metallic image and its portrayal of the rise and fall of universal empires and he drew a direct parallel between the two. Dan 7:17, Dan 2:37- 44
   B. As the prophet witnessed the emergence of the 4th beast, in the midst of the 10 horns corresponding to the period of the divided kingdoms, **another kingdom is seen to arise,** at first smaller than the 10, but afterwards becoming more stout than they.
   And it was **diverse from them - for it had eyes - keen, shrewd, intelligent eyes - of a man, and** it had **a mouth** with which it **uttered proud sayings and put forth preposterous and arrogant claims.** It was the activity of this little horn kingdom that gripped the prophets attention, grieving and troubling his spirit.
   Dan 7:7, 8, 15, 16, 19-25

II. Rome in Transition - Paganism Cloaked in the Garments of Christianity, called Roman Catholicism and Papal Rome

A. As Daniel witnessed the emergence of this little horn kingdom, he stood in awe of its nature, its character, & its activity, for it arose with the power and authority of a political kingdom, for it plucks up, destroys, & roots-out 3 of the original 10 kingdoms. Yet, it is religious in nature, in character, and in activity, as it wars against the saints of the Most High, and thinks to change that law of the Most High which is set in time. Furthermore, **it is seen to continue in this activity for a time, times, and a dividing of time.** Dan 7:23-25

This same power is represented in Rev 13 :1-7 **"And there was given unto him a mouth speaking great things and blasphemies; and power was given unto him to continue forty and two months.** And he opened his mouth in blasphemy against God - to blaspheme His name, and His tabernacle, and them that dwell in Heaven. And it was given unto him to make war with the saints, and to overcome them."

This same time period is brought to view in Rev 12:6 in which **the church** (woman) is said to **flee into the wilderness to escape this persecution** to a place prepared for her by God **for a thousand two hundred and threescore days,** described in Rev 12:14 as **a time, and times, and a half a time.**

What are these three time periods indicating how long **this little horn kingdom persecutes the saints of the Most High?** In order to understand the reckoning of these 3 time periods there are 3 things we need to consider:

1. **In biblical reckoning of time one year consist of 360 days with 30 days in each month.** Compare Gen 7:11, 8:4, 7:24
2. **The use of the term time refers to one year.** The historian Flavius Josephus tells us that Nebuchadnezzar was insane for 7 years, while Daniel 4 portrays him as being in this condition for 7 times. Works of Josephus page 316, Antiquity of the Jews book 10, chapter 10, section 6, Dan 4:16, 25
3. **In Biblical reckoning of time-prophecies God shows that a day stands for a year.** Num 14:34, Ezek 4:6

Applying these three points stated above we get:

Time	= 1 year	= 360 days
Times	= 2 years	= 720 days
Half a Time	= 1/2 year	= 180 days
Total	= 3.5 years	= 1260 days
42 months	= 30 X 42	= 1260 days
1260 days		= 1260 days

Applying the day for a year principle means that 1260 days represents 1260 years of prophetic-time.

B. Does human history reveal the rise of such a religio-political power, a church employing the arm of the state, to impose her teachings and dogma upon the people? Does the record expose the atrocities of this power heaped upon the saints of the Most High God for over 12 long centuries? And how, pray tell, has the record portrayed the presumptuous claims of this power to that which is the prerogative of Deity alone? Does the record not also show her blasphemies against God, His tabernacle, and those who dwell in Heaven?

1. To all these questions, we answer affirmative. "That the Church of Rome has shed more innocent blood than any other institution that has ever existed among mankind will be questioned by no Protestant who has a complete knowledge of history." Testimony of W. E. Lecky, DR, Chapter 7

2. This Church of Rome is called the Roman Catholic Church, Papal Rome, or the Papacy, which is Rome under popes.
Both Pagan and Papal Rome are chronicled in records of both human and biblical history as persecuting the saints of God. **In Rev 13, we witness Satan's accomplishment of his ultimate objective in the creation of paganism - the cloaking of his pagan sun worship in the garments of Christianity and coming in the name of Jesus.** This is Roman Catholicism, **clearly identified** in the book "The Two Babylons" by Alexander Hislop, **to be Christianized paganism, or Spiritual Babylon.**

3. "It requires but little historical investigation to prove that Rome, both in times of antiquity and during the Dark Ages, carried forward a work of destruction against the church of God.
Abundant evidence can be given showing that prior to and following the great work of the Reformation, **wars, crusades, massacres,**

inquisitions, and persecutions of all kinds were the methods adopted to compel all to submit to the Roman yoke. …….. **When confronted by heresy, she does not content herself with persuasion; arguments of an intellectual and moral order appear to her insufficient, and she has recourse to force, to corporal punishment, to torture.**" DR Chp 7

C. The period of 1260 years of papal supremacy commenced with the decree of Justinian, emperor of the eastern division of Rome. The edit of the emperor, dated AD 533, made the bishop of Rome head of all the churches, decreeing his preeminence over the bishop of Constantinople. But the edit could not go into effect until opposition of the Arian Ostrogoths, the last of the 3 horns to be plucked up, was removed in Rome. Sending his general, Belisarius, to accomplish this work in AD 538, the emperor curtailed the effective opposition of the Arians, though the date AD 553 marked the final uprooting of the Ostrogoths. Hence, the date for the beginning of papal supremacy is AD 538. From that year, the 1260 years reach to 1798.

III. Attack Upon the Law of God

A. "**And he ……… shall think to change times and laws**" Set in the context of warring against the saints of the Most High and speaking "great words against the Most High," this statement appertains to an assault by this power upon the law of the Most High. Dan 7:25

1. **The apostle Paul speaks of the activity of the papacy** when he warns the early Christian Church not to look for Christ 2nd coming before "there come a falling away first, and **the man of sin, the son of petition** be revealed; **who opposeth and exalted himself above all that is called God, or that is worshiped; so that he as God sitteth in the temple of God, showing that he is God.**" 2 Thes 2:1-4

2. "**Only by changing God's law could the papacy exalt itself above God;** whosoever should understandingly keep the law as thus changed would be giving supreme honor to that power by whom the change was made. **Such an act of obedience to papal laws would be a mark of allegiance to the pope in place of God**" (GC, Chapter 25, pg. 446)

   a. "The papacy has attempted to change the law of God. The 2nd commandment, forbidding image worship, has been dropped from the law, and the fourth commandment has been so changed as to authorize the observance of the first instead of the seventh day as the Sabbath", and the tenth commandment has been divided to preserve the number. "But papist urge," that the 2nd commandment "is unnecessary, being included in the 1st, and that they are giving the law exactly as God designed it to be understood. This cannot be the changed foretold by the prophet." But, the "intentional, deliberate" "change in the fourth commandment exactly fulfills the prophecy. For this, the only authority claimed is that of the church. Here the papal power openly sets itself above God." GC, Chapter 25, pg. 446

b. **"Roman Catholics acknowledge that the change of the Sabbath was made by their church, and declare that Protestants by observing the Sunday are recognizing her power"** (GC tip 25, p 447)

"As the sign of the authority of the Catholic Church, papist writers cite **"the very act of changing the Sabbath into Sunday, which Protestants allow of; ...... because by keeping Sunday, they acknowledge the church's power to ordain feast and to command them under sin."**

H. Tuberville, An Abridgment of the Christian Doctrine - page 58. What then is this change of the Sabbath, but the sign, or mark of the authority of the Roman Church - "the mark of the beast'? GC, Chapter 25, p 447, 448

"Romanist declare: **"The observance of Sunday by Protestants is a homage they pay, in spite of themselves, to the authority of the (Catholic) Church"**

> "The observance of Sunday by Protestants is a homage they pay, in spite of themselves, to the authority of the (Catholic) Church"

(Mgr Segur, Plain Talk About the Protestantism of Today, page 213, GC Chp 25, p 448

IV. Judgment, Judgment, and Judgment.

A. While beholding the activity of the papacy, the prophet sees 3 scenes of judgment (Dan 7:21, 22).

1. When the **Ancient of Days comes and the judgment is set** Dan 7:9, 10.
2. During the 1000 years following Christ's 2nd Advent when **judgment is given to the saints of God** Rev 20:1-4, 1 Cor 6:2, 3

DANIEL 7 PART 2

3. After the 1000 years when Christ and the saints return to the earth, the wicked are resurrected to be arraigned along with Satan and his demons in the executive judgment. Then **the time will come when the saints possess the kingdom.** Rev 20:5-15

B. **Until the Ancient of Days came.** GC, Chapter 28, page 479-484

This judgment scene portrays the **Ancient of Days, God the Father, taking His seat as the presiding official.** And **holy angels** as ministers and witnesses, in number "ten thousand times ten thousand, and thousands of thousands," **attend this great tribunal. The judgment is set and the books are opened.** In describing the same scene in Revelation, John adds:

"Another book was open which is **the book of life: And the dead were judged out of those things that were written in the books, according to their works."** Rev 20:12, Ecc 12:14, Matt 12:36, 1 Cor 4:5, Dan 7:10

1. **Three books are opened in the judgment:**
   a. **The book of life** which contains the names of all who have professed faith in Christ and have entered the service of God Ex 32:31-33, Phil 4:3, Rev 21:27
   b. **The book of remembrance,** in which are **recorded the good deeds of "them that feared the Lord, and thought upon His name"** - words of faith, acts of love, deeds of righteousness, Temptations resisted, every evil overcome, words of tender pity, every sacrifice and every suffering endured for Christ's sake." Mal 3:16, Neh 13:14, Ps 56:8, GC, Chapter 28
   c. **The book of the record of the sins of men.** "Entered with terrible exactness, every wrong word, every selfish act, every unfulfilled duty, every secret sin, with every artful dissembling.

   Heaven sent warnings or reproofs neglected, wasted moments, unimproved opportunities, the influence exerted for good or evil with its far-reaching results, all are chronicled by the recording angel." Isa 65:6, 7, Jer 17:1, 2:22, GC, Chapter 28

2. **"One like the Son of Man came with the clouds of heaven, and came near the Ancient of Days,** and they brought Him near before Him." Thus is described Christ's coming to the judgment to receive dominion and glory and a kingdom as our Mediator and Advocate in the judgment.
   Dan 7:13,14, 1John 2:1, 1Tim 2:5, Heb 9:24, 7:25

As the books are opened in the judgment, the lives of all who have believed on Jesus come in review before God. **"Beginning with those who 1st lived upon the earth, our Advocate presents the cases of each successive generation, and closes with the living. Every name is mentioned, every case closely investigated. Names are accepted, names are rejected.** When any have sins remaining upon the books of record unrepented of and unforgiven, their names will be blotted out of the book of life, and the record of their good deeds will be erased from the book of God' remembrance." John 12:47,48, Eze 18:21-24, Rev 3:5, GC, Chapter 28, Ex 32:33

3. "Thus is presented to the prophet's vision the great and solemn day when the character and the lives of men should pass in review before the judge of all the earth, and to every man should be rendered according to his works." (GC pg. 479). **When Christ ceases this ministry, every case will be decided. He will have determined those who shall be the subjects of His everlasting kingdom.** Thus "there was given Him dominion, and glory, and a kingdom." Dan 7:13, 14, Rev 22:11, 12

THIS IS THE INVESTIGATIVE JUDGMENT!

C. **And Judgment was Given to the Saints.** 1 Cor 6:1-4 1 Cor 6:1-4, GC page 660

1. **"Do ye not know that the saints shall judge the world?"** **"Know ye not that ye shall judge angels?"** (1 Cor 6:2, 3)
   This judgment takes place after the 2nd coming of Christ and during the one thousand years between the general resurrection of the righteous and the general resurrection of the wicked (John 5:28, 29, Rev 20:1-7). **In this judgment the saints in union with Christ determine the punishment to be apportioned to the wicked for their sins.** The one thousand year period in which this judgment takes place is called the millennium. Rev 20:1-7

THIS IS THE MILLENNIAL JUDGMENT!

D. **And the Time Came that the Saints Possessed the Kingdom**
   1. **At the end of the one thousand years, Christ and the saints return to the earth.** The general resurrection of the wicked takes

place and Satan is thus loosed for a little season. Having subjects to tempt and control, the devil makes preparation for his final attempt to war against Christ. In the mean while, Christ descends upon the Mount of Olives and purifies the ground, and it becomes a great plain before Him. The Holy City comes down from Heaven and settles on the purified ground. At the invitation of Christ, the righteous enter the Holy City. Zechariah 14:3, 4, GC chapter 42

His preparations made, Satan marshals the vast throng of the wicked over the broken desolate earth to surround the Holy City. **As the wicked surround the city, Christ's final coronation takes place above the heights of the city, and the wicked are arraigned before the judgment seat of Christ on charge of high treason against the government of God.** In a panoramic view all the issues involved in the great controversy between Christ and Satan is witnessed by the onlooking multitude. **After every question is answered, every lying excused is dispelled, and every deception is exposed, every knee shall bow in acknowledgment God's justice in His dealings with sin.** Then fire and brimstone will rain down from God out of Heaven to destroy the wicked, root and branch - Satan the root, his followers the branches - and will purify the heavens and the earth from all traces of sin. A new heaven and a new earth will fill the place of the old, and will be the home of the righteous. God will move His throne from Heaven, beyond the Constellation Orion, to the earth. The earth, where the Son of God lived, suffered, and died will become the center of the Universe. Rev 20:7-15; 21:8; Zech 14:3-5, 9, 12; Mal 4:1-3; 2Pet 3:9-14

THIS IS THE EXECUTIVE JUDGMENT!

Chapter X

REVELATION 12 - PAGANISM AND THE EARLY CHRISTIAN CHURCH

I. The Old Testament as the foundation of the New Testament is elevated and magnified in it.
   A. The New is in the Old contained
      The Old is in the New explained

      The New is latent in the Old
      The Old is patent in the New

      The New is in the Old concealed
      The Old is in the New revealed

      The New is in the Old enfolded
      The Old is in the New unfolded

   B. That which troubled, perplexed, and grieved the prophet Daniel in the vision of Dan 7 concerning the 4th beast, the 10 horns, and the little horn who continued until destroyed in the burning flame is expounded upon in the line of prophecy symbolized in Rev 12:1 to Rev13:18
      1. Three great powers are portrayed representing 3 great systems of false religions, all of which promote the teachings of

Babylonian Mysticism. Revelation 12 examines the first of these false religions, which is known as paganism.

II. The Church in Transition and Her Seed
   A. **In Gen 3:15, the 1st promise of hope, of redemption, of salvation, and recovery from the ruin of sin is proclaimed, revealing the great controversy between Christ and Satan.**
   B. In Rev 12, we see the conflict as it began in Heaven and as it continues upon the earth, and we witness the ratification of this promise of hope, of redemption, of salvation, and recovery from the ruin of sin.
   C. **An Elucidation of the Symbols**
      1. A woman symbolizes a church. Isa 4:1-4
         A pure woman, depicted in modesty and chasteness, represents a church that holds to the truth as it is in Jesus, a church that walks in the light of the law of God. Rev 12:1, 17; 2 Cor 11:2; Ps 19:7, 8; Ps 1; 1 Pet 2:5, 9-12; 3:1-4
         An impure woman, depicted as a harlot, decked in jewels from her head to her toes, represents an apostate church, a church which by virtue of its illicit relations with the world misrepresents the truth and promotes corrupt and false doctrines Rev 17:3-6, 15, 18, Eze 23:2-4, Isa 3:16-24, Hosea 2
      2. **The woman is seen standing upon the moon, a symbol of the Old Testament Mosaic Era, the foundation upon which the church is built.**
         In types and symbols, in ceremonies, in feast and celebrations, in the history and economy of God's chosen people - the OT Era was the shadow of the cross cast as the Sun of Righteousness rose upon it from eternity in the future. At high noon, the time of the outshining glory of the Sun, **the Messiah came and we transitioned to the New Testament Era** - when type met antitype, when the shadow met the substance that cast the shadow. Thereafter, the light of the glory of Christ illuminates the past, the present, and the future.
      3. **The crown of 12 stars symbolizes the 12 apostles.**
      4. **The seed of the woman** with whom she travailed in birth to be delivered, who was to rule all nations with a rod of iron, who was caught up to God and His throne **is none other than the Christ, the Messiah.** Gen 3:15, 22:8-18, Gal 3:16, Ps 2:7-9, Eph 4:7, 8

5. Thus, the symbolic representation of the woman in Rev 12 portrays the period of time just before the opening of the Christian Era, when the church was earnestly longing for and expecting the advent of the Messiah, and extending to the full establishment of the Christian Church with its 12 apostles, who were called, trained, mentored, ordained and sent forth by Christ Himself (Matt 4:18-22, Luke 5:1-11, 27-32, John 1:35-51, Matt 10).

III. **The Great Red Dragon**
   A. **Primarily represents Satan** "that old serpent called the Devil ….." (Rev 12:3, 4, 9; Gen 3:15)
   B. **Secondarily represents the earthly power that stood ready as the agent of Satan to destroy Christ as soon as He was born - Pagan Rome in the person of Herod the Great.**
   (Rev 12:4 (last part), Matt 2:16)
   1. The 7 crowns located on the dragon's heads signify the period of time during which pagan empires still bore sovereign sway over the earth. The pagan Roman head is thus singled out.
   2. The 10 horns correspond to the period of the divided kingdoms, which, in this prophecy is yet future when the crowns shall shift from the heads to the horns. Dan 7:7, 8, 23, 24, Rev 12:3, Rev 13:1

IV. **A Celestial Conflict Continued upon the Earth**
   A. **The controversy between Christ and Satan is represented as beginning in Heaven: "And there was war in Heaven." Christ, whose name was Michael before the incarnation, stood at the head of the loyal angels and met Satan and the disloyal angels on their own level, pitting strength against strength, might against might, employing no power that Satan could not exercise. Michael prevailed against Satan, and the rebellions angels were cast out of Heaven.** Rev 12:3, 4, 7-9,
   Dan 9:21, 10:12, 13, 20, 21. After this world was created, Satan carried forward his warfare against God by usurping the dominion of this world from Adam and becoming the prince and ruler of it.
   Job 1:6-12, John 14:30, 16:11
   1. **When the Son of God entered this world as the Christ, Satan personally embarked upon continuing that warfare begun in**

Heaven, intending to succeed on earth to redeem his defeat in Heaven. Matt 4:1-11
2. Though all the weapons of hell were arrayed against Him, **Christ died to self, depended wholeheartedly upon His Father, and, by faith and implicit trust in the Word of God, triumphed over the devil and made a show of him openly.** Col 2:15
3. Satan sought to turn Christ away from the cross. Seeing that he could not, he led sinful men to exhibit fiendish mockery, derision, and exultation in crucifying Him; and this with the cooperation of Pagan Rome. Having succeeded in laying Christ in the tomb, Satan determined to keep Him there. Such is the insanity of sin. No power in earth or hell could hold Christ under the power of death. **Having lived a perfect and sinless life in this world, Christ, by His death on Calvary Cross, regained the lost dominion. The words, "It is finished," sounded Satan's deathnell. So unveiled were the devils deceptions, so disclosed were his true character as a liar and murderer, that all sympathy for him was cast down and cast out of the minds of the loyal universe** (Rev 12:10; John 12:31; 19:30).

> "The words, "It is finished," sounded Satan's deathnell. So unveiled were the devils deceptions, so disclosed were his true character as a liar and murderer, that all sympathy for him was cast down and cast out of the minds of the loyal universe"

Yet, Satan was not destroyed, sin had not yet run its full course. Satan had yet another deception to bring forth.

B. **The controversy between Christ and Satan, which began in Heaven and continues upon the earth, centers in the law of God.**
When Satan led Adam and Eve to sin against God, disobeying His requirements, he exulted in his supposed demonstration of the impossibility of man to keep the commandments of God. **Christ, in 33 years of the human experience, unveiled this deception and refuted Satan's lying claims by demonstrating that mankind could live in perfect harmony with the law of God.**
1. All during Christ's earthly life, Satan tempted Him to disobey God, to doubt God's love, to question God's requirements. He moved

upon sinful men, who were the representatives of God's chosen people, to entrap Christ and accuse Him of being a lawbreaker - a Sabbath breaker - to malign His motives and His character, all the while they were trampling its precepts underfoot. Mark 2:23-28, 3:1-6, Matt 15:1-9. **Christ steadfastly upheld the precepts of God's Holy Law in their true light, demonstrating that the ruling principle that governed the keeping of the law is love.** Matt 22:34-40, Gal 5:14, James 2:8-12, Deut 6:4-9, 10:12-19, 30:6 Luke 10:25-37. 1 John 3:13-18, 4:7-11, 16-20, Ex 20 The 1st four precepts of the law are summed up in love to God supremely, and declares our relationship to God. The last 6 precepts are summed up in love to one another impartially, and declares our relationship to one another. "**By His life and His death, Christ proved that God's justice did not destroy His mercy, but that sin can be forgiven, and that the law is righteous, and can be perfectly obeyed**" (Desire of Ages, p 762)

2. "Another deception was now to be brought forward. Satan declared that mercy destroyed justice, that the death of Christ abrogated the Father's Law." "**The very means by which Christ established the law Satan represented as destroying it**" (DA, p 762).

"That the law which was spoken by God's own voice is faulty, that some specification has been set aside, is the claim that Satan now puts forward. It is the last deception that he will bring upon the world. He needs not to assail the whole law; if he can lead men to disregard one precept, his purpose is gained. "For whosoever shall keep the whole law, and yet offend in one point, is guilty of all." (DA, Chp 79, pg. 762; James 2:10)

"**By substituting human law for God's law, Satan will seek to control the world.**" Dan 7:25, Rev 13:8, 11-17, DA , p 763

C. "The warfare against God's Law, which was begun in heaven, will be continued until the end of time. Every man will be tested. Obedience or disobedience is the question to be decided by the whole world. **All will be called to choose between the law of God and the laws of men.** Here the dividing line will be drawn."

"**Every character will be fully developed; and all will show whether they have chosen the side of loyalty or that of rebellion**" (DA, page 763).

REVELATION 12

V. **When the Religion of the Empire is Threatened**
   A. **No longer able to war directly against Christ, the malignity, hatred, and venom of Satan is directed against His Church.**
   "Woe to the inhabiters of the earth and of the sea! for the devil is come down unto you, having great wrath, because he knoweth that he hath but a short time. And when the dragon saw that he was cast unto the earth, he persecuted the woman which brought forth the man child" (Rev 12:12, 13). After the stoning of Steven in 34 AD, the Jews launched a great persecution against the Christian church at Jerusalem and the disciples were scattered abroad. The 70 week, 490 day/yr prophecy appointed to the Jews to remain God's chosen people expired, and the gospel was given to the Gentiles. Saul of Tarsus was converted and became the apostle to the Gentiles, and in his lifetime, the gospel was given to the entire then known world (Acts 7:59-8:1; 9:1-6, 10-22; Dan 9:24-27; Col 1:23). So effectively did the apostles spread the gospel that it made inroads into the courts of royalty in pagan Rome and began to sweep away its superstitions, overturn its idols, and dismantle its temples.
   The religion of the empire was threatened, and Satan moved upon paganism to summon her forces to stamp out and to destroy Christianity. GC, Chapter 2, p 39)
   B. The fires of persecution broke forth upon the early Christian Church.
   "Christians were stripped of their possessions and driven from their homes ... "Great numbers sealed their testimony with their blood. **"Noble and slave, rich and poor, learned and ignorant, were alike slain without mercy"** (GC, p.39). "These persecutions, beginning under Nero about the time of the martyrdom of Paul," continued for centuries. "Christians were falsely accused of the most dreadful crimes and declared to be the cause of great calamities - famine, pestilence, and earthquakes." "They were condemned as rebels against the empire, as foes of religion, and as pest to society. Great numbers were thrown to wild beast or burned alive in the amphitheaters. Some were crucified; others were covered with the skin of wild animals and thrust into the arena to be torn by wild dogs. Their punishment was often made the chief entertainment at public fetes. Vast multitudes assembled to enjoy the sights and greet their dying agonies with laughter and applause." GC, Chapter 2, Heb 10;32, 11:36, **"And they overcame him**

by the blood of the Lamb and by the word of their testimony, and they loved not their lives unto death." Rev 12:11

C. Allusion is made to the continued warfare of paganism against the church beyond the period of the sovereignty of the pagan empires.

Then, Satan will have achieved his ultimate objective in the creation of paganism, the cloaking of his pagan sun worship in the garments of Christianity and coming in the name of Jesus. Papal Rome became the agent of Satan to heap even greater atrocities upon the Christian Church then that done by Pagan Rome. Rev 12:6, 14, 15. The Protestant Reformation grew broad and deep in the 16th century cutting short papal persecutions. Then, in the 17th century, God's providence opened up the new world of the Americas to provide sanctuary for His people from the persecutions of the old world. Thus, "the earth helped the woman, and the earth opened her mouth." Rev 12:16, Matt 24:21, 22. Finally, through the persecutions of a supposedly Christian nation and the agencies of Satan promoting the teachings of Babylonian Mysticism, Satan makes war against God's remnant church who keep the commandments of God, and have the witness of the Holy Spirit in the gift of prophecy. Rev 12:17, 19:10

Chapter XI

REVELATION 13 - ANTICHRIST - THE LEOPARD BEAST PAGANISM CLOAKED IN GARMENTS OF CHRISTIANITY

I. **Identifying the Leopard Beast of Rev 13**
   A. "And I stood upon the sand of the sea, and saw a beast rise up out of the sea, having 7 heads and 10 horns, and upon his horns 10 crowns, and upon his heads the name of blasphemy. And the beast which I saw was like unto a leopard, and his feet were as the feet of a bear, and his mouth as the mouth of a lion: and the dragon gave him his power, and his seat, and great authority." Rev 13:1, 2. From our study of Dan 7, Chapter 8 - V, we concluded that the non-descript beast with the 10 horns represents Pagan Rome, and that it manifested the characteristics of:
   1. The leopard beast with the 4 heads in the philosophical reasoning and wisdom of Greece
   2. The feet of the bear of Persia, which was despotic and trampled the law of God underfoot.
   3. The blaspheming mouth of Babylon with its counterfeit system of religion.

4. And when the little horn arose among the 10 horns and plucked up 3 of the 10, Pagan Rome gave place to Papal Rome (Chapter 9-II).
   B. The composite beast of Rev 13 is similar in description to the dragon beast of Rev 12, clearly identified to be Pagan Rome. Like the dragon it had 7 heads, 10 horns, and crowns. Only the crowns have shifted from the heads to the horns, and upon the heads is the name of blasphemy.
      1. **The shifting of the crowns indicate a progression in time** from the period of the sovereignty of the pagan empires **to the period of the divided kingdoms.**
      2. **The replacing of the crowns upon the heads with the name of blasphemy indicates a change in the character of the beast.**
      The religion of the dragon beast was paganism. The religion of composite beast is paganism cloaked in the garments of Christianity Chapter VI. According to the Scriptures, blasphemy is the act of a mortal being making himself out to be God, or claiming that which is the prerogative of deity alone. (Luke 5:21; John 10:33).
   C. "And the dragon (Satan and Pagan Rome) gave him (the composite beast) his power, and his seat, and great authority. Rev 13:2
      What power succeeded Pagan Rome? The decree of Justinian, emperor of the eastern division of Rome, in AD 533, signaled the passing of the power, seat, and authority of the empire from pagan rulers into the hands of the ecclesiastical rulers of the Church of Rome and the bishop of Rome, who came to be called the pope of the Roman Catholic Church. But the decree could not go go into effect until the rule of the Ostrogoth, in the 7 hilled city of Rome, was broken. This was not achieved until AD 538.
   D. The dragon beast and the composite beast are similar because they both symbolize the Roman Empire. The dragon represented Rome in her pagan form; the leopard represents Rome in her professedly Christian form, the papacy - an ecclesiastical despot claiming universal dominion over all temporal and spiritual affairs. **The empire did not perish, it simply underwent a transformation.** The pope who calls himself King and Pontifex Maximus, is Caesar's successor.

II. The Little Horn of Dan 7 and the Leopard Beast of Rev 13
   A. In Chapter IX Parts II we identified the little horn as the ecclesiastical power that would arise to rule the world for 1260 years, and who

would employ the arm of the state to impose his will and dogmas upon the world.

Six points will suffice to show that the little horn and the leopard beast are one and the same power.

1. **Both spake great words and blasphemies against God.**
   Dan 7:25, Rev 13:6
2. **Both made war against the saints and overcame them.**
   Dan 7:21, Rev 13:7
3. **Both arose out of the ruins of the pagan form of the Roman Empire** during the period of the divided kingdoms.
   Dan 7:8, 20, 23, 24, Rev 13:2
4. **Both continued in power for 1260 years.** Dan 7:25, Rev 13:5
5. At the end of the 1260 years the saints, times, and laws, shall be taken out of the hand of the little horn, "the judgment shall sit, and they shall take away his dominion" (Dan 7:26).
6. At the end of the same period, he who tortured, persecuted, and led into captivity, shall go into captivity; he who massacred and killed with the sword, must be killed with the sword. Rev 13:5, 10 **Both of these specifications were fulfilled when Napoleon sent his General Berthier into Rome to overthrow the Papacy in February of 1798.**

III. Prophecies Fulfilled - Extracts from Roman Catholic Writers

A. "The priest hold the place of the Savior Himself, when, by saying 'Ego te absolvo' (I thee absolve), he absolves from sin ….. To pardon a single sin requires all the power of the omnipotent God …… But what only God can do by His omnipotence, the priest can do by saying 'Ego te absolvo a peccatis tuis' ………. Innocent III has written: "Indeed, it is not too much to say that in view of the sublimity of their office the priest are so many gods." "But our wonder should be far greater when we find that in obedience to the words of his priest - Hoc Est Corpus Meum (This is my body) - God Himself descends on the altar, that He comes whenever they call Him …… and places Himself in their hands, even though they be His enemies ….. He remains entirely at their disposal: They move Him as they please ……. shut Him up in the tabernacle, or expose Him on the altar, or carry Him outside the church; they may, if they choose, eat His flesh, and give Him for food to others. Oh, how very great is their power, says St Laurence Justinian, speaking of the priest." "A word falls from their lips and the body of Christ is there substantially formed from the matter of bread, and the incarnate Word descended from heaven, is found really present on the table of the altar." "Thus the priest may, in a certain manner be called the creator of the Creator ……. For the transubstantiation of the bread requires as much power as the creation of the world." Alphonso de Liguori, Dignity and Duties of the Priest page 26, 27, 32-36, AC 666 page 147-149, 159-161

B. All names which in Scripture are applied to Christ, ………all the names are applied to the pope." "Thou art the shepherd, thou art the physician, thou art the director, thou art the husbandman; finally, thou art another god on earth." "The pope is the supreme judge of the law of the land ……. He is the vicegerent of Christ, who is not only a priest forever, but king of kings, and lord of lords." "The pope is crowned with a triple crown, as king of Heaven and king of earth, and king of the lower regions."
(Contrary to Scripture - 1Tim 6:14-16, Isa 44:6-8, 45:18-22, 46:9-11)
Bible Readings for the Home - Kingdom and Work of Anti Christ, page 205

C. "They have assumed infallibility, which belongs only to God.
They profess to forgive sins, which belongs only to God. They profess to open and shut heaven, which belongs only to God. They profess to be higher than all the kings of the earth, which belongs only to God. And they go beyond God in pretending to loose whole nations from their oath of allegiance to their kings, when such kings do not please them. And they go against God, when they give indulgences for sin. This is the worst of all blasphemies." Adam Clark on Dan 7:25 BRH page 206

IV. Papal Rome - Christianized Paganism

A. Much of the cherished terminology of the Roman Catholic Church antedates the Christian Era.
  1. The title Pontifex Maximus or Supreme Pontiff, which originally meant "Bridge Builder," but now simply denotes the Pope, was used to describe the office of the head of pagan cults centuries before Emperor Constantine recognized Christianity as a legal religion. The Caesars were Roman Pontiffs. AC 666, page 146
  2. The term diocese, meaning the territory under a bishop's jurisdiction, was originally an administrative unit devised by Emperor

Diocletian, who was, incidentally, noted for his persecution of Christians. AC 666, page 146

3. From where did the Catholic church receive the name cardinals? The pagan high priest had a college of councilors who helped him in temporal matters as well as religious matters. They were called cardinals, the priest of the hinge (The 2 Babylons page 210, 211).

4. The sisterhood of nuns is derived from the roots of Babylonian sun worship. Just as the vestal virgins or the other virgins of the sun were shut up in a house for women, so are these poor women of the Catholic Church cloistered. AC 666 pp 162

5. The Roman Catholic Church has clearly identified Mary with the Queen of Heaven, the pagan mother goddess. In the doctrine of the immaculate conception, Mary is said to have been conceived in her mothers womb without the stain of original sin, ostensibly that she might be the mother of God. They teach that Mary is the mother of God and even call her by the ancient name, "The Queen of Heaven." AC 666 page 164

6. Rome teaches that death is not an end of life, but a metamorphosis in which the divine spark of life transitions from the physical to a spiritual life. This is the teaching of immortality of the soul, first taught by Satan to Eve "Ye shall no surly die," and is promoted by pagans as the foundation and center of their whole belief and worship. Just as pagans believed in the burning place of torment, limbo, and a place for good spirits to go, so Rome teaches a hell fire, purgatory (the place of purification), and paradise. Rome holds festivals to honor the departed spirits of loved ones, and claim to have members in their church who receive messages from the dead. In paganism this occult practice was called necromancy. Instead of calling those who perform these abominations mediums, they are called mystics (AC 666 page 168-170).

> "Rome teaches that death is not an end of life, but a metamorphosis in which the divine spark of life transitions from the physical to a spiritual life."

8. The rosary is no invention of the papacy. It is of the highest antiquity and almost universally found in pagan nations. AC 666 page 171-172

9. Transubstantiation, the blasphemous claim that a priest can change a wafer into the flesh of Christ and wine into His blood, is the same doctrine taught by ancient Babylon. The pagan high priest and kings impersonated their deities by pretending they were Baal's incarnate, who had power to turn the round disk into their chief god, the sun, the ruler of the zodiac. AC 666, page 159, 160

B. **This is the crowning work of Satan in the development of paganism, the cloaking of his Babylonian sun worship in the garments of Christianity and coming in the name of Jesus. With this development arose the second of three great false religious systems, Roman Catholicism,** which also persecuted the followers of Christ and carried forward the teachings of Babylonian mysticism.

Chapter XII

DANIEL 8 - PAGANISM & THE PAPACY TRAMPLING UNDERFOOT THE SANCTUARY

I. The 2nd of a Series of Visions - The Rise & Fall of Universal Empires
   A. Again by the principle of enlargement through repetition the Divine Teacher increases our knowledge. **Increasing light is shed upon the earlier prophecies revealing greater details, refining the information already given, and enlarging upon it.**
   Daniel received this vision in the 3rd year of the reign of Belshazzar, acting king of Babylon, co-regent with his father Nabonidus.
   Daniel was at Shushan when he saw the vision in the palace which is in the province of Elam, by the river of Ulai. And he identified it as being like the vision he had in chapter 7 (Dan 8:1).
   Babylon was in its decline, hence is not symbolized in the vision.
   B. **"The ram which thou saweth having 2 horns are the kings of Media and Persia."** Dan 8:20
      1. There is no room for speculation or misrepresentation here.
      The 2 horns represented the 2 nations so named. The higher of the 2 horns which came up last symbolized Persia, which at first was simply an ally of the Medes, but later became the predominant power of the empire. The direction which the ram pushed denoted the direction in which it carried forward its conquest. **No earthly power could stand before it as it marched toward the exalted**

position to which the providence of God summoned it. He did according to his will, and **the ram waxed great.**

Dan 8:3, 4, 20, Isa 45 :1-6, Jer 51:8, 9, 11-14, 28-31, 39, 56-58

C. **"And the rough goat is the king of Grecia (Greece): And the great horn that is between his eyes is the first king."** Dan 8:21

Greece lay west of Persia and attacked from that direction with such marvelous celerity of movement, with such swiftness as to be depicted as touching not the ground. The battles between the Greeks and Persians were said to be exceedingly fierce. "Alexander 1st vanquished the generals of Darius III at the River Granicus in Phrygia. He next routed Darius III at the passes of Issus in Cilicia, and afterwards defeated him on the plains of Arbela in Syria. **This latter battle occurred 331BC and marked the fall of the Persian Empire. "And there was none that could deliver the ram out of his hand. Therefore the he goat waxed very great."** At the height of his power, while yet going forth conquering and to conquer, Alexander met with sudden death brought on by a fever after a drunken debauch. His sons were soon murdered, his family became extinct, and the chief commanders of his army who had gone into different parts of the empire as governors of the provinces, assumed the title of king, and immediately began to war among themselves to such a degree that within a few years after Alexander's death the number was reduced to four. The prophecy declares that, when the 1st horn is broken, 4 kingdoms shall stand up out of the nation, but not in his power. Chapter 8, part IV, Sec C; Dan 8:8, 21, 22

D. **"In the latter time of the 4 kingdoms,** when transgressors are come to full, **a king of fierce countenance , and understanding dark sentences, shall stand up."** "Out of one of them shall come forth **a little horn, which waxed exceeding great**, toward the south, and toward the east, and toward the pleasant land. **And it waxed great even to the host of heaven."** Dan 8:23-25, Deut 28:47-57

   1. Although this power is not named, from the line of succession of the earthly powers introduced thus far, we are clearly dealing with the rise and fall of universal empires from Medo-Persia and onward. There is also a direct parallel between this vision and the visions of Dan 2 & 7. **The power that succeeded Greece was Rome.** Earthly governments are not introduced into prophecy until they become in some way connected with the people of God. Rome became connected with the Jews by the famous Jewish League of

161BC. But, 7 years before this in 168 BC Rome had conquered Macedonia, the western horn of the goat, and went forth to new conquest in the other directions.

Rome conquered Syria in 65BC and made it a province, hence waxed toward the east. Judea is called the pleasant land and was made a province of Rome in 63BC. Rome made Egypt a province of its empire in 31BC and hence waxed toward the south. The transition from the pagan to the papal phase of the empire is suggested by the change in the activity from Dan 8:9 to 11. In verse 9 it is seen to wax exceeding great in political conquest towards the remaining divisions of Alexander's empire and Judea as noted above. In verse 10 & 11 it is seen not to be waging military warfare against nations, but spiritual warfare against the followers of Christ, and even against Christ Himself.

Verse 10 refers to the activity of both Pagan (100 - 313 AD), & Papal Rome (538 AD and beyond), for both persecuted the saints of God. Verse 11 refers to **paganism crucifying Christ,** and the **papacy exalting itself above Christ to supplant His Priesthood & Ministry, & cast His Sanctuary to the ground.** The Little Horn waxed great, event to the host of heaven; and it cast down some of the host and of the stars to the ground,
And stamped upon them. 2 Thes 2:3, 4, Dan 8:11

Host - the followers of the power/person with whom the term is associated. In this case, it is Christians

Stars - the ministers, leaders, apostles of Christ

"**And Rome waxed great, even to the Christians; and it cast down some of the Christians and the Apostles to the ground, and stamped upon them.**" Dan 8:10, 24

II. The Little Horn in its Papal Phase Warring Against the Christ.
   A. "Yea, he magnified even to the Prince of the host, and by him the daily was taken away, and the place of His sanctuary was cast down …….. and it cast down the truth to the ground; and it practiced, and prospered. ………. How long the vision, the daily and the transgression of desolation, to give both the sanctuary and the host to be trodden underfoot? …., Unto two thousand and three hundred days; then shall the Sanctuary be cleansed." Dan 8:11-14

1. Since the host identified above refers to Christians, it follows that **The prince of the host is Christ**.
2. **Daily** - occurs in the Old Testament 102 times, according to the Hebrew concordance, and in most instances it is **rendered continual or continually. But, continual what?** The term must be applied in the context in which it is used. In verse 11 the term is used in reference to the Prince of the host , for, it was when the daily is taken away, that the place of his (the prince of the host - Christ's) sanctuary was cast down. The place to which Christ ascended after His resurrection was "the right hand of the throne of the Majesty of the heavens; a minister of the sanctuary, and of the true tabernacle, which the Lord pitched and not man (Heb 8: 1-6; Dan 8:11, 25). In verse 13 a question is asked about the vision concerning the daily and the transgression of desolation; to give both the sanctuary and the host to be trampled underfoot. In both the construction and the context, the term **daily refers to a desolating power like the transgression of desolation.** Since the vision in question concerns the activity of paganism from Medo-Persia to Rome - in both its pagan and papal phases - it follows that, **if the transgression of desolation refers to Papal Rome, then the daily refers to that continual desolation that preceded Papal Rome,** who conferred upon her the power, the seat, and great authority of Pagan Rome (Rev 13:2; Dan 8:23-25).

> "
> if the transgression of desolation refers to Papal Rome, then the daily refers to that continual desolation that preceded Papal Rome, who conferred upon her the power, the seat, and great authority of Pagan Rome
> "

3. **Transgression of desolation** - a term ascribed to Rome in its papal phase to describe its actions in warring against God. It is a desolating power achieving its aims by reason of transgression.
Once transformed from paganism to the papacy, Rome set up its own priestcraft and ministry in the place of Christ's priest hood and ministry and cast down the place of Christ's sanctuary. The Apostle Paul describes this activity as **the working of the man of sin, the son of perdition .... "Who opposeth and exalteth himself above all that is called God, or that is worshiped; so that he as God sitteth in the temple of God, showing that he is God"** (2 Thes 2:4)

B. "An host was given against the daily by reason of transgression, and it cast down the truth to the ground; and it practiced, and prospered" (Dan8:12)
   1. **It was under Rome that paganism underwent a transformation, appeared to be vanquished or taken away, and supplanted by the Catholic Religion.** The barbarians that subverted the western division of the Roman Empire in the changes, attrition, and transformations of those times, became converts to the catholic faith, and the instruments of the dethronement of their former pagan religion. **Though conquering Rome politically, they were themselves vanquished religiously by the theology of Rome, and became the perpetuators of the same empire in another form.** This was brought about by reason of transgression, that is, by the mystery of iniquity, a human power ascribing to itself that which is the prerogative of Deity alone. The truth is by it hideously caricatured, loaded with traditions, turned into mummery and superstition, cast down and obscured. It practiced its deceptions on the people, practiced its schemes of cunning to carry out its own ends and to aggrandize its own power. It prospered in making war upon the saints; in exercising sovereign rule over the nations; and it has accumulated the wealth of the world for nearly 12 long centuries. But, it shall be broken without hands, given to the burning flames, and perish in the the consuming glories of the 2nd Advent of our Lord.

III. **The Longest Time-Prophecy Introduced**
   A. **"How long the vision, the daily and the transgression of desolation, to give both the sanctuary and the host to be trodden under foot?"**
      1. The vision that God gave to Daniel concerns the activity of the pagan empires - Medo-Persia, Greece, and Rome - and the activity of Papal Rome - that ecclesiastical despot who succeeded Pagan Rome. The 2300 year prophecy is about the duration of the vision, and not the duration of the time of the ruin and desolation of the sanctuary. Yet, it specifically addresses the question of when the sanctuary is to be restored for its cleansing. The restoration of the sanctuary is based on the principle of the first and the last mention, and thus addresses the restoration of both the earthly-Old Covenant sanctuary at the beginning of the prophetic period, and

the heavenly-New Covenant sanctuary at the end of the period (1 Cor 15:46-48) Since the coming of the Messiah marked the transition from the literal to the spiritual and from the Old Covenant to the New Covenant, we should expect the restoration of the literal earthly sanctuary to take place before the advent of the Messiah, and the restoration of the spiritual heavenly sanctuary to take place after the coming of the Messiah. Jeremiah describes how God raised up Nebuchadnezzar, king of Babylon, as His agent to punish Jerusalem and bring desolation and ruin upon the earthly sanctuary that would last 70 years from 606 BC (Jer 25:8-11). Isaiah and Ezra describe how the Lord raised up Cyrus to initiate the decree for the restoration of the earthly sanctuary in 536 BC (Isa 44:28; 45:13; Ezra 6:14), and Artaxerxes to finalize the decree for the restoration of the earthly sanctuary and Jerusalem in the fall of 457 BC (Ezra 6:14; 7:21-26). Dan 9:25 tells us that 49 years from 457 BC, the earthly sanctuary and Jerusalem would be rebuilt. The earthly sanctuary was rebuilt by 408 BC, but again destroyed for the last time, in AD 70, following literal Israel's rejection and crucifixion of the Messiah in AD 31. With the termination of the 70 weeks prophecy in AD 34 (Dan 9:24), the Jews cease to be God's agents for the spreading of the gospel (Mat 23:37, 38). Literal Israel was replaced by Spiritual Israel, the Christian Church, and the earthly sanctuary ministry by Christ's ministry in the heavenly sanctuary. Yet, the destruction of this earthly sanctuary was delayed to give opportunity for the Jews to be converted to Christianity. This last earthly sanctuary was destroyed in AD 70 when Titus laid seige to Jerusalem.

From 457 BC, the 2300 year prophecy terminated in the year AD 1844, declaring "Then shall the sanctuary be cleansed" (Dan 8:14). Since the earthly sanctuary was destroyed in AD 70, and the literal was replaced by spiritual in AD 31 with the crucifixion of Christ, this cleansing, in 1844, could only have reference to the heavenly sanctuary, of which the earthly sanctuary was a type (Ex 25:8, 9; Heb 8:1, 2, 5; 9:11).

B. **"Unto two thousand and three hundred days, then shall the Sanctuary be cleansed."** This answer shows that the central point of concern is the cleansing or restoration of the sanctuary. **But, what is the sanctuary?** When Daniel sought understanding of the vision, the angel **Gabriel stood before him with the commission to "make this man to understand the vision."** Gabriel told Daniel that "at the time of the end shall be the vision, ... wherefore shut thou up the vision; for it shall be for many days" (Dan 8:17-26)

When Daniel heard these words he "fainted, and was sick certain days; .... was astonished at the vision, but none understood it" (Dan 8:27).

1. **What was it about the vision that the prophet failed to understand?** Certainly not the powers represented by the ram, the he goat, and the little horn, introduced with the same line of succession as portrayed in Dan 2 & 7, two of whom are clearly identified. No, the elucidation of these is too plain to escape understanding. **It was something about the sanctuary being cast down and trodden underfoot and the 2300 years before which it could be cleansed that smote the prophet with this sickness.** Why? Because the time for the earthly sanctuary to be restored was only 70 years from 606BC, and he could not reconcile this long period of time with Jeremiah's prophecy of Israels 70 years of captivity. Daniel erred in applying the 2300 years to the cleansing of sanctuary as opposed to the duration of the vision. He failed to see how that it addressed the time of the restoration of both the earthly and the heavenly sanctuary. **The 2300 day/year prophecy commences with the decree for the return of Literal Israel from Babylonian captivity to rebuild/restore the temple and Jerusalem** (Dan 9:24, 25, Ezra 6:14), to repair the damage done by the Babylonians (Neh 2:17-20, Isa 58:12-14).

   The ending brings us to the time when Spiritual Israel, the Christian Church, comes out of Spiritual Babylon to restore all things (Mal 4:5, 6,) - the true temple service (Rev 11:1), and to repair the breach done by Spiritual Babylon. Isa 58:1-4; 6-14; Dan 8:11, 25

IV. **What Shall Be in the Last End of the Indignation?**
   A. **God told the Jews that He would pour out His indignation upon them in consequence of their apostasy** in going beyond the limits of divine forbearance by **bowing before Satan's system of sun worship.** Eze 21:24-32, 8:13, 15; Jer 7:17, 20

   Thus He gave direction concerning the **"profane, wicked prince of Israel"** …….. "Remove the diadem and take off the crown … I will

overturn, overturn, overturn, it: and it shall be no more, until He comes whose right it is; and I will give it Him. Eze 21:25-27. It was God who called for the diadem to be removed and the crown to be taken off the head of a chosen but rebellious people. Then He demonstrates how that behind the scene of human events, He is in control, as He allows the sovereignty of this world to pass into the hands of nations who do not love, worship, and obey

Him - Babylon, Medo-Persia, Greece, and Rome - until He comes whose right it is. Spiritual Israel has taken the place of literal Israel but are subject to earthly powers until He comes whose right the kingdom of this world is. Then the indignation will cease.

Chapter XIII

WHAT IS & WHY - THE SANCTUARY?

I. Thy Way O God is In the Sanctuary!
   A. David affirmed "Thy way, O God, is in the Sanctuary: Who is so great a God as our God?" Ps 77:13, 63:1-2, 68:24. 96:6
   Asaph declared how perplexed and disturbed he was in trying to live a godly life when he beheld the corruption, the pride, the prosperity of the wicked. **So disturbed was he, that he almost gave up on the way of the cross - until he went into the Sanctuary of God: Then understood he the end of the wicked.** Ps 73:1-17
   How is it with you and I? Has our feet well-nigh slipped? Have we given up on the way of the cross? Have we gone into the Sanctuary of God that we may understand?
   If you would behold God's power and great glory, you must look for Him in the Sanctuary. Ps 63:1, 2
   If you would behold the goings of God, even the goings of …. my King, then you must look for Him in the Sanctuary. Ps 68:24
   Honor and Majesty are before Him: Strength and Beauty are in HIs Sanctuary. Ps 96:6

II. What is the Sanctuary as Revealed in the Scriptures?
   A. **The apostle Paul tells us that the term sanctuary first refers to the tabernacle built by Moses as a pattern of heavenly things, called a worldly sanctuary, the sanctuary of the Old Covenant.** Heb 9:1-10, 8:5
   "The Lord spake unto Moses saying" …… "And let them make Me a sanctuary; that I may dwell among them. According to all that I show thee, after the pattern of the tabernacle, and the pattern of all

the instruments thereof, even so shall ye make it." At least 7 times the Scriptures declare that the sanctuary of the Old Covenant was made after the pattern of the Heavenly, and thus was of no human devising. Ex 25:8, 9, 40; 26:30; 1Chron 28:9-12, 19; Acts 7:44; Heb 8:4, 5

   B. **The Apostle Paul tells us that the term secondarily refers to the true tabernacle in Heaven, which the Lord pitch, and not man - the sanctuary of the New Covenant.** Heb 8:1, 2, 7-13, 9:8-12, 24

III. Why the Sanctuary and what is a sanctuary?

   A. With the entry of sin - a strange, foreign, intruding element was introduced into God's perfect Universe, and an attack was made upon the Creator, upon His creation, and upon the very laws by which creation is enabled, upheld, sustained, governed, and its very existence promoted. Satan had been so highly honored, and "all his acts were so clothed with mystery, that it was difficult to disclose to the angels the true nature of his work. Until fully developed, sin would not appear the evil that it was. "It is impossible to explain the origin sin so as to give a reason for its existence. …. Could excuse for it be found, or cause be shown for its existence, it would cease to be sin" (GC, pg. 492)

What was the Sovereign of the Universe to do?

A stage was provided in which the Sovereign God would allow Satan's play and counter-play of sin to manifest it's outworking's, and allow Him to reveal to the Universe the outworking of His love in a work of atonement by which the Godhead would provide a new and living way to recover mankind from the ruin of sin. For the stage, God created the earth and laid its foundation forever. The earth is the court of the sanctuary where the Son of man would present Himself as mankind's Substitute and Surety of deliverance from sin - "the Lamb of God, which taketh away the sin of the world" (John 1:29).

The sanctuary is the 2 apartment tabernacle in heaven, which the Lord pitched, where He pleads the blood of His holy life and sacrificial death in behalf of all who receive Him as their personal Savior. Here, in panoramic view, the issues involved in the great controversy between Christ and Satan is witnessed by the onlooking universe of free moral beings who remained faithful and loyal to God (Isa 45:18; Heb 8:1, 2).

      1. God's work of atonement would involve 3 phases to completely recover mankind from the ruin of sin - ministries in the court, and

in the holy place and the most holy place of the tabernacle. Only after the final work in the most holy place can it be said that the atonement is complete, for **atonement** means to make man again **at-one-with** God.

B. **What is a sanctuary?** A sanctuary is a place set apart for sacred purposes. It is a sacred place of refuge and protection. Notice what the Scriptures declare our place of refuge and protection to be:

"God is our refuge and strength, a very present help in trouble." Ps 46:1. And the invitation is "Come unto to Me, all ye that labour and are heavy laden, and I will give you rest …..and ye shall find rest unto your souls. Matt 11:28

God invites us to find in Christ our Sanctuary. As we study into the subject of **the sanctuary**, we discover that it **is a compacted prophecy of Christ, revealing the attributes of His character; His holy life & sacrificial death, His triumphant resurrection & glorious ascension, His triumphal entry into the heavenly tabernacle to minister as our great High Priest in a 2 phase work of atonement; and His glorious appearing as King of Kings and Lord of Lords** (1 Tim 6:15; Rev 19:16).

> As we study into the subject of the sanctuary, we discover that it is a compacted prophecy of Christ

In every sacrifice **Christ's death was shown.**
In every cloud of incense **His righteousness ascended.**
By every jubilee trumpet **His name was sounded.**
In the awful mystery of the holy of holies **His glory dwelt.** AA pg 14
In the Sanctuary we shall **behold Christ as Prophet, Priest, and King.** Deut 18:15-19, Heb 8:1-5, 9:11, 12, 24

IV. The Structure of the Sanctuary

A. There was a building divided into two apartments by a rich and beautiful veil of the gorgeous colors of blue, scarlet, purple, and white fine twine linen, hung on 4 pillars overlaid with gold and set in 4 sockets of silver. Figures of cherubic were woven into this veil in threads of gold and silver representing the angelic host connected with the work of the Sanctuary, who are ministering spirits of God's people on earth. Heb 1: 13, 14

The walls of the tabernacle were made of upright boards overlaid with gold, giving the building the appearance of solid gold. The inner covering of the tabernacle was of the same tapestry as the veil, followed by a covering of goat's hair, then a covering of ram's skin dyed red, and after that an outer covering of sealskin (badgers), so arranged as to afford complete protection. The door of the 1st apartment was of blue, scarlet, purple, and white fine twine linen wrought with needlework and hung on 5 pillars of gold, set in 5 sockets of brass. The sacred building was enclosed in an open space called the court of the tabernacle, which was enclosed by a wall of white fine twine linen curtain hangings suspended from pillars of brass about half as high as the tabernacle. The entrance to the court, like that of the 1st and 2nd apartments of the tabernacle, was from the eastern end - the direction from which the Sun of Righteousness arises with healing in His Wings, and was a gate of the curtain hangings of blue, scarlet, purple, and white fine twine linen, hung on 4 pillars overlaid in brass and set in 4 sockets of brass. Ex26, 36, 38:9-20, PP page 347

B. **The colors** of the curtains hanging, the veil, the door, the gate, and the inner coverings; **and the metals** that the pillars and walls were overlaid with and the threads made with - **depicts the attributes of Christ's character in His human experience.**

Blue .... Obedience .... Num 15:38-40
Scarlet .... Sacrifice/Blood .... Lev 17:10-14
Purple .... Royalty .... John 19:2, 3
White .... Righteousness .... Rev 19:8, Isa 61:10
Gold .... Faith & Love 1Pet 1:7-9
Silver .... The Word of God .... Ps 12:6
Brass .... Strength/Endurance .... Deut 33:25

- An alloy of copper and zinc formed in the furnace, brass depicts **Christ in the furnace of affliction** in His earthly sojourn, **made perfect through suffering** (Heb 2:9, 10; 5:8-10; Phil 2:8-10).

As blue mixed with scarlet produces purple, so also, **as the children of God walk in the footsteps of Christ's obedience and self-renouncing, self- sacrificing love, are they fitted to become members of the royal family of God** (1Pet 2:9, 21-24; 3:18; 4:1, 2, 12, 13, 19).

V. **The Furnishing of the Sanctuary**
   A. Nearest the entrance to the gate of the court stood the brazen altar of burnt offering where every sacrifice made by fire unto the Lord was consumed. Between the altar and the door of the tabernacle was the brazen laver for washing. Here the priest had to wash himself before ministering either in the tabernacle or at the brazen altar, less he die. Ex 27:9-18, 30:18-21
      1. Every furnishing in the court was of brass signifying the perseverance of Christ in duty as He tread the winepress alone, and was made perfect by the things that He suffered (Isa 63:1-5; Heb 2:10).
   B. **"In the 1st apartment, or holy place,"** was the table of shewbread **to the north** upon which were 12 cakes in 2 stacks of 6, baked fresh each Sabbath and sprinkled with frankincense. These were held over from Sabbath to Sabbath, kept continually before the presence of the Lord, typifying Israel's complete & continual dependence upon God for temporal and spiritual bread. "The loaves that were removed, being accounted holy, were eaten by the priest." **To the south was the seven branch golden candlestick** with its 7 lamps kept continually burning and shedding their light by day and by night. **Before the veil was the golden altar of incense,** beyond which in the most holy, was the immediate presence of God. Heb 9:2, Ex 26:33, 35, 30:1-7, PP page 348
   C. **In the 2nd apartment, or most holy place or holy of holies, was the ark made a depositary for the 2 tables of stone upon which God Himself inscribed His 10 Commandment Law on blue sapphire stones** (Ex 24:10, 12). "Above the ark, and **forming a covering for the sacred chest, was the the mercy seat,"** "surmounted by 2 cherubim, one at each end, and all wrought in solid gold." They faced each other with one wing stretched on high, the other folded over the body in token of "the reverence with which the heavenly host regard the law of God and their interest in the plan of redemption." Between the cherubim and above the mercy seat was **the Holy Shekinah, the visible manifestation of the glory of God**, before which none but the High Priest could minister and live (GC page 412, 414; PP page 348, 349; Ex 26:33, 34; Lev 16:16, 17, 29-34; Heb 9:1-3)

VI. **What was the Spiritual Significance of the Earthly Sanctuary?**
   A. **The court represents the earth where Christ in 33 years of the human experience generated human redemption** by His holy life & sacrificial death, and by His triumphant resurrection & glorious ascension, and that without us. On earth He was not a priest, but was that Prophet of whom Moses spoke. Heb 8:4, 5, Deut 18:15-19
      1. **The brazen altar,** where every sacrifice made by fire unto God was offered up, **represents the cross of Calvary where Christ offered sacrifice, Himself the Lamb.** Heb 9:11-14, 10:1-4, 8-14
      2. **The brazen laver typifies the washing which Christ underwent in the watery grave of baptism** to fulfill all righteousness, which **pointed forward to His death, burial, and resurrection, and that higher cleansing from sin - the baptism of the Holy Spirit.** Thus, as the priest must wash before ministering at the brazen altar or in the tabernacle, so Christ washed before ministering at the cross and in the heavenly tabernacle (Matt 3:11-17; Rom 6:3, 4; John 3:3, 5-8; Acts 1:4, 5).
   B. **The holy place of the tabernacle of the congregation represents the holy place of the heavenly sanctuary, where Christ ascended** after His resurrection to minister "at the right hand of the throne of the Majesty in the heavens" as our great high priest (Heb 8:1, 2; Heb 9:11, 12, 24). It would appear from Rev 4 that the **table of shewbread represents the place of God's throne in the holy place** before which was the **7 lamps of fire** which correspond to the **7 branched golden candlestick** and **represents the full and complete activity and work of the Holy Spirit** (John 14:16, 17; 16:7-14; Acts 1:4, 5; 2:1-4; Rev 4:5)
   C. **The most holy apartment of the earthly sanctuary represents the most holy apartment of the heavenly sanctuary** into which Christ passed when the temple of God was opened in Heaven and the ark of the testament was seen. This apartment was **only open** or entered once a year **on the day of atonement. The ark of the covenant and the mercy seat above which was the holy Shekinah glory indicates the location of the throne of God in the most holy apartment of the heavenly sanctuary,** and shows it to be established upon mercy and justice. Ps 85:10, 89:14 This apt was **entered October 22, 1844 when the 2300 day/year prophecy ended and type met anti-type as we entered the Antitypical Day of Atonement for the cleansing of the sanctuary.**

WHAT IS & WHY - THE SANCTUARY?

VII. Was the Earthly Sanctuary made after the Pattern of That Which Actually Physically Existed in Heaven?

  A. Moses made the portable Earthly Sanctuary after the pattern that was shown him on Mt Sinai. Solomon built the permanent Earthly Sanctuary in Jerusalem after the pattern that God gave to David. Paul teaches that the pattern was the true Sanctuary which is in Heaven. And John testifies that he saw it in Heaven. Ex 25:8, 9, 40, 1 Chron 28:9-13, 19, Heb 8:1-5, Heb 9:11, 24, Rev 4:1-5, 8:3, 11:19, GC page 414-415

Notice this quote from the Spirit of Prophecy:

> "I was also shown a sanctuary on earth containing two apartments. It resembled the one in heaven, and I was told that it **was a figure of the heavenly. The furniture** of the first apartment of the earthly sanctuary **was like that in the first apartment of the heavenly.** The veil was lifted, and **I looked into the holy of holies** and saw that **the furniture was the same as in the most holy place of the heavenly sanctuary."** Early Writings page 252-253, 32, Heb 9:1-11, 24

LET NO ONE SPIRITUALIZE AWAY THE REALITY OF THE EXISTENCE OF THE TRUE SANCTUARY WHICH THE LORD PITCHED AND NOT MAN. TRUE, THERE ARE GREAT AND FAR-REACHING SPIRITUAL OBJECT LESSONS TAUGHT IN EVERY PIECE OF FURNITURE, IN EVERY WOVEN CURTAIN, AND ALL THE INSTRUMENTS THEREOF: YET, THE HEAVENLY SANCTUARY IS BOTH PHYSICAL AND MATERIAL IN ITS EXISTENCE - PITCHED FOR THE REVELATION OF CHRIST JESUS AND HIS WORK OF ATONEMENT TO RECOVER HUMANITY AND THE UNIVERSE FROM THE RUIN OF SIN! IT MUST ALSO BE REALIZED THAT A MERE THEORETICAL OR THEOLOGICAL KNOWLEDGE OF THE SANCTUARY THAT DOES NOT PRODUCE A VITAL CONNECTION AND RELATIONSHIP WITH CHRIST IS INSUFFICIENT FOR THE SAVING OF THE SOUL. FOR CHRIST IS INDEED EVERYTHING TO US!
John 14:6, 13, 5:38-40, Col 3:1-3, 11, 1:27, 1Cor 1:30, Acts 4:12, 5:

Chapter XIV

THE SANCTUARY MINISTRY IN THE HOLY PLACE

I. Where did the Apostle Paul say that Christ went after His resurrection, and for what purpose?
   A. Paul declares that, when Christ ascended to heaven, "We have such an high priest, who is set on the right hand of the throne of the Majesty of the heavens; A minister of the sanctuary, and of the true tabernacle, which the Lord pitched, and not man." "But Christ being come an high priest of good things to come, by a greater and more perfect tabernacle, not made with hands, that is to say, not of this building; Neither by the blood of goats and calves, but by His own blood He entered in once into the holy place, having obtained eternal redemption for us" (Heb 9:11, 12). "For Christ is not entered into the holy place made with hands, which are the figures of the true; but into heaven it self, now to appear in the presence of God for us" (Her 9:24). "Let us come boldly unto the throne of grace, that we may obtain mercy, and find grace to help in the time of need" (Heb 4:16).

II. What Ministries were Foreshadowed in the holy place of the Earthly Sanctuary?
   A. Throughout the year there were three main services performed daily, **called the daily ministration.**
      1. **The evening and morning sacrifice of the whole burnt offering upon the brazen altar.** Ex 29:38, 39, 42-44

THE SANCTUARY MINISTRY IN THE HOLY PLACE 93

2. **The evening and morning offering of sweet incense upon the golden altar.** Ex 30:1, 6-10
3. **The special offering for individual sins.** Lev 4

III. **What was the Nature and Significance of the Evening & Morning Sacrifice of the Whole Burnt Offering?**
   A. "The whole burnt offering had its origin at the gate of the garden of Eden, and extended to the cross ..... **The entire sacrifice was laid upon the altar and burned, typifying not only a surrender of sin, but a consecration of the entire life to the service of God**" (CS page 132) "Every morning and evening a lamb of a year old without blemish, was burned upon the altar, with its appropriate meat offering, thus **symbolizing the daily consecration of the nation to Jehovah, and their constant dependence upon the atoning blood of Christ**" (PP page 352, Gen 4;1-7, 8:20-22, Ex 29:38-46, Rom 12:1).
   B. What great truth is here taught about the altar of burnt offering?
   IT WAS AN ALTAR OF CONTINUAL ATONEMENT!

IV. **What was the Nature and Significance of the Evening & Morning Offering of Sweet Incense?**
   A. This was a work that none but the High Priest could perform. He alone, being in the fullest since a type of Christ, our Great High Priest, could offer **sweet incense** upon the golden altar, which **typified the adding of the fragrant incense of Christ's Righteousness to the prayers of the saints to render them acceptable before God.** Ex 30:1, 6-8, Rev 8:3, 4
      1. Evening and morning the High Priest burned sweet incense upon the golden altar, a perpetual incense before the Lord. "**The incense ascending with the prayers of Israel represents the merits and intercession of Christ, His perfect righteousness, which through faith is imputed to His people, and which can alone make the worship of sinful beings acceptable to God.**" PP page 353, Ex 30:7, 8
   B. What great truth of redemption is here taught about the altar of sweet incense?
   IT WAS IN ALTAR OF PERPETUAL INTERCESSION?

V. **Notice How the Beauty of God's Plan of Redemption is Magnified Before Us!**

A. "Before the veil of the Most Holy was an altar of perpetual intercession; before the veil of the Holy, an altar of continual atonement. **By the blood and by the incense God was to be approached - symbols pointing to the Great Mediator, through whom sinners may approach Jehovah, and through whom alone mercy and salvation can be granted to the repentant, believing soul."** PP, page 353 Notice the accountability & responsibility of the Giver and receiver of free moral agency that enables human redemption.

"The intercession of Christ in man's behalf in the sanctuary above is as essential to the plan of salvation as was His death upon the cross" (GC page 489). **By His death** He reconciles humanity to God, placing all in the position whereby we can approach God and be saved. **By His High Priestly Ministry** He intercedes in behalf of those who receive Him as their personal Savior and then fits them to live in the sight of a Holy God.

THINK THIS THROUGH MEDITATE AND REFLECT UPON IT!

VI. **What was the Nature and Significance of the Offering For Individual Sins?**

A. This was the most important part of the daily ministration. **Day by day the repentant sinner brought his offering - a lamb, a bull, a goat, two wild turtle doves, or two pigeons - according to his wealth, position, or ability.** If he were unable to afford the former, and was too destitute or feeble to catch two wild turtle doves, a mere hand full of flour would satisfy the Lord's claim. **God made provision for all** (CS pg. 124, 128, 129; Lev 4:1-7; 5:1-7, 11-13; GC, pg 418).

"**The repentant sinner brought his offering to the door of the tabernacle, and, placing his hands upon the victims head, confessed his sins, thus in figure transferring them from himself to the innocent sacrifice."** Then he would slay the victim, for without the shedding of blood there is no remission, no putting away, and no forgiveness of sins. "**The blood, representing the forfeited life of the sinner, whose guilt the victim bore," was caught in a basin and "carried by the priest into the holy place and sprinkled before the veil that separated the holy place from the most holy place," beyond which was the law that the sinner had acknowledge breaking** (PP, pg. 354, GC, pg. 418)).

Thus his sins were in figure transferred from the slain victim by the blood to the sanctuary. In some cases the blood was not taken into the holy place; but then the flesh was to be eaten by the priest in the holy place, for God had given it unto the priest in such cases to bear the iniquity of the people, to make atonement for them. **Both ceremonies alike symbolized the transfer of sins to the sanctuary.** Lev 6:25, 26, 10:17-20

The sinner had yet another task to perform. While the priest was administering the blood, the sinner was to pick all the fat from the organs of the sin offering and give it to the priest when he returned to be burned upon the brazen altar. Nothing was to remain but ashes.

VII. What Great and Far-Reaching Spiritual Truths Were Taught in The Daily Ministration?

A. **A substitute was accepted in the sinners stead, but, only as the sinner saw in the substitute a type of the Messiah, the Lamb of God, was there any efficacy in his going through this - God's appointed way - to receive the forgiveness of sins.** John 8:56; Gen 22:7, 8; Heb 10:5-10; John 1:29; Rev 13:8; Gen 4:3-7

　1. As the sinner lifted his own hands to slay the innocent victim, the truth was indelibly impressed upon his mind that his sins would make him a partaker in slaying the Lamb of God, the promised Messiah, the Christ. Thus was foreshadowed **the Great Atoning Death of Christ**, the Son of Man, lifted up on Calvary's Cross:
- **Satisfying completely the claims of God's Holy Law.**
- **Paying in full the wages of sin in the sinners stead.**
- **Bridging the gulf that sin had made between God and man, that man might again be at-one-with his Maker and God.**

B. The **confessed sins** of the sinner were in figure transferred from him to the substitute, **in actuality transferred from him to Christ;** by the blood of the victim **transferred** in figure to the earthly sanctuary, **in actuality to the heavenly sanctuary by the blood of Christ.** Yet, the **sins remained,** accumulating upon the veil separating the holy place from the most holy place in the earthly sanctuary, and **accumulating in the book of records in the heavenly sanctuary. Though pardoned, the sinner was not yet entirely released from the condemnation of**

the law. Lev 4:5, 6, 16, 17, Isa 65:6,7, 59:12, Jer 17;1, 2, 2:22, Acts 3:19, GC page 420

C. **Fat represents sin. The sinner picking all the fat from the organs of the victim typified his searching of his heart for sins unconfessed, sins unrepentant of.** The burning of the fat on the brazen altar foreshadowed the final consummation of sin, where nothing remains but ashes. Ps 37:20, Mal 4:1-3

VIII. **What Shall We Say About the Work of Atonement? Was it Complete At the Cross? Was it Complete at the End of the Daily Ministration?**

A. **At the cross a full and complete sacrifice for sin was wrought out by Christ - Himself a Perfect Atoning Sacrifice** - and that without us. But the effecting of the atonement in the human heart was not complete at the cross.

1. **"Atonement" means to make us again "at-one-with" God. The death of the sacrifice did not make the atonement, neither** does it save the sinner or confer upon him the the free gift of righteousness that all must have to be saved. No, the death, following the holy life without spot or blemish, **serves to reconcile us to God and to place us in the position whereby we can be saved. We are saved by Christ's life, the merits of which are applied to the repentant sinner; and we receive the atonement by the ministration of His blood in the heavenly sanctuary.** In order to receive Christ's life we must go beyond His death to His resurrection, for, **"if Christ be not raised, our faith is vain, we are yet in our sins, and they who are fallen asleep in Him are perished."** 1Cor 15:14, 17,18. In order **to receive the atonement,** we must go beyond the resurrection to Christ's high priestly ministry in the heavenly sanctuary. Rom 5:9-11, Lev 17:11, Heb 9:11-14, 22, 23, 4:14-16

2. **Though wrought out full and complete without us, salvation will never become our without us. The will must consent, faith must lay hold of Christ as a personal Savior** in order for us to appropriate unto ourselves the merits of His holy life and sacrificial death, the only remedy for sin. Only then can God make effectual in man Christ's perfect righteousness and make man again at one with Him. Hence it was expedient that Christ go and send the Holy Spirit in His stead (John 14:26, 16:7-14, Eph 4:30).

THE SANCTUARY MINISTRY IN THE HOLY PLACE 97

The Holy Spirit comes with the fullness of divine power to lead & guide us into all truth, and to effect in us all that has been generated by Christ. It is the Spirit who leads us to confess and repent of sins that we may be justified. He comes with the fullness of divine power to enable and empower to victory over sin that we may be sanctified. Then the Spirit will Imprint the character of Christ upon His followers and seal us unto that great day of redemption (1 Cor 2:9-11; Eph 4:30)

HENCE THE WORK OF ATONEMENT WAS NOT COMPLETE AT THE CROSS!

B. **The ministration in the daily secured pardon for sins confessed and repented of, yet the sins still remained. Christ,** typified by the priest taking the blood of the innocent victim into the Holy Place, **pleads His blood in behalf of the guilty sinner.** No human eye sees the hand that lifts the guilt from the burdened, weary soul as **Jesus imputes His righteousness to him,** places His righteousness against the account of the confessed and repented sins. By faith the sinner is forgiven. By faith he seeks to grow up unto the measure of the stature of the fullness of Christ, the meanwhile being kept from sinning by the sanctifying work of the Holy Spirit imparting to him the righteousness of Christ. **He is pardoned, forgiven, justified, and accepted just-as-if he had not sinned, yet, his sins still remain. A transaction occurs in which he exchanges his sinful life for Christ's righteous life and receives the gift of the Holy Spirit who comes with the fulness of divine power to grow him up into his new life in Christ, and he moves from death to life, from sin to holiness, from transgression and rebellion to obedience and loyalty.** Wonder, O Wonder - God's reversal of the fall - moving us towards His rest! Zech 3:1-5, Isa 61:10, Rom 8:1, 2, 4:20-25, Ps 32:1, 2, 5, 6 Heb 4:3, 10

1. **The blood ministry in the first apartment deals with sins that are past, sins committed, sins that no human hand can turn back the clock to undo.** Christ, lifting His nailed scarred hands pleads in our behalf and claims us as His own, engraved upon the palms of His hands. In the place of our sinfulness He imputes His righteousness, places His holy life and sacrificial death against the account of our sinfulness and we are forgiven. **But God's plan of redemption comprehends more than the mere forgiveness of**

man's sins. It comprehends man's complete recovery and restoration from the ruin of sin that man might perfectly reflect the character of our Lord and Savior, and be sealed unto the great day of redemption. Isa 49:16, Heb 5:8-10. 6:1, 7:11, 19, 9:13, 14

2. For sins that are past God invites us to **come boldly unto the throne of grace to receive mercy.** Yet, the invitation does not stop with mercy; it goes on to invite us to **find grace to help in the time of need.** Heb 4:16

By "the exceeding riches of His grace" (Ehp 2:7), God desires to "quicken us together with Christ" (Eph 2:5) and to raise us up to "sit together in heavenly places in Christ Jesus" (Eph 2:6 He wants to grant us "according to the riches of His glory, to be strengthened with might by His Spirit in the inner man;" that Christ may dwell in our hearts by faith; that we, "being rooted and grounded in love, may be able to comprehend …. what is the breadth, and length, and depth, and height; and to know the love of Christ, which passeth knowledge," that we "might be filled with all the fullness of God" (Eph 3:16-19). This fullness is **"Christ in you, the hope of glory"** (Col 1:27). This is Bible Sanctification: **The supernatural work of the Holy Spirit transforming our nature, purifying our heart, keeping us from sinning, and impressing the character of Christ upon us.** Far greater than the mere forgiveness of our sins, God desires to completely recover us from the ruin of sin and to restore us to be in perfect harmony and accord with His character, and love. To enable us to attain to this experience is the object of the Godhead's three phase work of atonement (Rom 8:1-10, 13; Acts 3:19-21). Only then, do we enter into God's rest (Heb 4:3-5, 9, 10; Matt 11:28).

> *Far greater than the mere forgiveness of our sins, God desires to completely recover us from the ruin of sin and to restore us to be in perfect harmony and accord with His character, and love.*

3. "The Blood of Christ, pleaded in behalf of the penitent believers (in the holy place), secured pardon and acceptance with the Father, yet their sins still remained upon the book of records (GC page 421).

"The Blood of Christ, while it was to release the repentant sinner from the condemnation of the law, was not to cancel the sin; it would stand on record in the sanctuary until the final atonement." PP page 357

There yet remains a final phase in Christ's work of atonement in the most holy apartment that will utterly remove and blot the sins forevermore that have gone before in confession and repentance and are then overcome! Isa 43:25, 44:22, Acts 3:19-21

HENCE THE WORK OF ATONEMENT WAS NOT COMPLETE AT THE END OF THE DAILY MINISTRATION!

"Having therefore, brethren, boldness to enter into the Holiest (The most holy apartment of the heavenly sanctuary) by the blood of Jesus, by a new and living way, which He hath consecrated for us, through the veil, that is to say, His flesh; And having a High Priest over the house of God; Let us draw near with a true heart full of assurance of faith, having our hearts sprinkled from an evil conscience, and our bodies washed with pure water.

Let us hold fast our profession of faith without wavering; (for He is faithful that promised;) And let us consider one another to provoke unto love and to good works; Not forsaking the assembling of ourselves together as the manner of some is; but exhorting one another; and so much the more, as ye see the day approaching." Heb 10:19-25, Heb 4:3-5, 9, 10

Chapter XV

THE SANCTUARY MINISTRY IN THE MOST HOLY PLACE

I. Why the Subject of the Sanctuary?
   A. "Yea, he (Rome) magnified himself even to the prince of the host (Christ Jesus), and by him the daily (paganism) was taken away, and the place of his (Christ's) sanctuary was cast down ..… How long the vision, the daily (continual desolation - paganism), and the transgression of desolation (the papacy), to give both the sanctuary and the host (worshipers of the living God) to be trodden under foot? Unto two thousand and three hundred days; then shall the sanctuary be cleansed. Dan 8:11-14

II. Questions Answered.
   A. We have answered the question **"What is the sanctuary?** Chp XIII
      1. **The tabernacle built by Moses after the pattern of the heavenly things shown him in Mt. Sinai, called the earthly sanctuary, the sanctuary of the Old Covenant.** Ex 25:8, 9, 8:5, 9:1
      2. **The tabernacle in heaven which the Lord pitched and not man, the sanctuary of the New Covenant.** Heb 8:1, 2, 6-13
   B. We have further seen that there are two divisions of ministration in the tabernacle of the sanctuary - a daily and a yearly. **In the daily:**
      1. The sacrifice of the whole burnt offering in the evening and morning typified the daily consecration of the life to God and Israel's constant dependence upon the atoning blood of Christ.

2. The evening and morning burning of sweet incense upon the golden altar typified worship of God in prayer through the merits and intercession of Christ, His perfect righteousness, which through faith is imputed to His people, and which alone can make the worship of sinful beings acceptable to God.
3. The service for the individual or congregation made provision for the confession and repentance of sins that the sinner(s) might be forgiven, justified, and accepted just-as-if they had not sinned. At the end of the daily ministry an atonement was made to secure pardon and acceptance of the people with the Father, yet their sins still remained. While the blood of Jesus "was to release the repentant sinner from the condemnation of the law," it "was not to cancel the sin" (PP, pg. 357) There remains yet a final phase in Christ's work of atonement that will utterly remove and blot out sins forevermore. This final work of atonement is the ministry of our High Priest in the most holy place for the restoration and cleansing of the sanctuary.

Anciently, this day of ministry was called the Day of Atonement (Lev 23:27-32). On October 22, 1844, when Christ commenced His final work of atonement, we entered the period of the Antitypical Day of Atonement (GC, pg. 418-419)

II. How was the Day of Atonement Foreshadowed in the Earthly Sanctuary?
A. So solemn was this period of time in the yearly experience of an Israelite that trumpets sounded the 1st day of the 7th month, "a sabbath memorial of blowing of trumpets" (Lev 23:24).

The sounding of the trumpets announced the near approach of the great Day of Atonement on the 10th day of the 7th month, and summoned the people to make solemn preparation for the day that would determine their destiny, for it was a day of judgment (Lev23:24-32). Then, on the 10th day, **the high priest**, dressed in his gorgeous robes with the breastplate of judgment bearing the names of the 12 tribes of Israel over his heart and the onyx stone with the names of the 12 tribes on his shoulders, **made atonement for the most holy place, the holy place, the court, and for all the people, to cleanse them of all sin that had gone before in confession and repentance during the daily ministry.** The people were required to cease from their own works and to fast and afflict their souls that their minds might be clear to follow their high priest in this closing work of atonement, or else they would be cut off and destroyed (Lev 23:29, 30).

Having first made an atonement for himself and his household, the high priest took of the congregation two kids of the goat for a sin offering and a ram for a burnt offering. To the door of the tabernacle he would bring them and would cast lots cast upon the goats, designating one for the Lord, the other for the scapegoat, Azazal. The high priest slew the Lord's goat for a sin offering for the people and passed into the holy place with the blood. There he obtained a golden censor from the golden altar full of hot coals, and a hand full of sweet incense. Just as he entered the most holy place, he placed the incense upon the hot coals and a cloud of fragrant incense rose up to shield him from the visible manifestation of the glory of God. He then sprinkled the blood upon and before the mercy seat (Lev 16:14). No man was allowed in the holy place while the high priest ministered in the most holy place, until he came out having made an atonement for the himself, for his household, and for all the congregation of Israel. Leaving the most holy, the high priest pauses to make an atonement for the golden altar, putting blood upon it's horns and sprinkling it 7 times upon the altar to cleanse it and hallow it from the uncleanness of the children of Israel (Lev 16:18, 19). When the high priest made an end of reconciling the most holy, the holy place, and the golden altar, he went out into the court figuratively bearing in his own person all the confessed sins of Israel out of the tabernacle. He then laid his hand upon the head of the scapegoat and confessed these sins over him. A fit man afterwards took the goat to a land not inhabited, a land of separation, bearing the sins away from the camp of Israel, nevermore to return. Lev 16:20-22, GC page 419, CS page 210 Going back into the holy place the priest laid off his gorgeous robes, and put on his other garments: Then coming again into the court he cleansed it from the defilement of sin. He burned the fat of the sin offering upon the brazen altar. The skin, the flesh, the dung, and the blood used to make the atonement were burned without the camp. Lev 16:23-28, CS page 210

III. **Thus was Foreshadowed in Types and Symbols the Final Events of God's Great Plan of Human Redemption!**
   A. **The parable of the 4 Watches in Mark 13:32-37 set the stage for trumpets sounding the return of Christ in the clouds of glory.**

THE SANCTUARY MINISTRY IN THE MOST HOLY PLACE 103

Four times God's people are admonished to watch for His return, and, associated with each watch is a coming. **We entered the evening watch** in February, 1798 when we entered the time of the end, the time beyond which the events surrounding Christ's 2nd Advent began to unfold (Dan 11:35; 12:4-13). Shortly after entering this period, God raised up individuals who, after studying the time prophecies of Daniel and holding to the commonly held view that the earth was the sanctuary, came to the conclusion that the 2300 year prophecy pointed to Christ's 2nd coming to purge the earth of sin. This led to an Advent awakening that spread throughout the world and reached its culmination following a spectacular display of falling stars that was seen all over the New England state in America on November 13, 1833. Seen by many as a harbinger of the end of the world and a fulfillment of Matt 24:29 and Rev 6:13, this gave impetus to the preaching of Christ's 2nd coming, and the warning of the 1st angel of Rev 14:6, 7 sounded with a loud voice. Coming 10 years before the expected end of the 2300 years, it was the antitype of the memorial of blowing of trumpets (Lev 23:24).

It was first believed that the decree of Artaxerxes, which finalized the commandment of God for reckoning the starting point of the 2300 years (Ezra 6:14), took place in the spring of 457 BC, which meant that Christ would come the spring of 1844. When the time passed and Christ did not come, the multitudes, who were caught up in the industrial revolution before the witness of the falling stars, but afterwards, jumped on the bandwagon out of hope of reward or fear of punishment, returned to their aspirations of acquiring land and temporal prosperity.

The coming associated with this watch is described in Rev 10, and **we transitioned to the midnight watch**. During this watch, the Lord showed His faithful followers that the decree of Artaxerxes went into effect in the fall of 457 BC, and He showed this to be consistent with the spring and fall feasts and celebrations of the Jewish economy. The spring feast pointed to events surrounding Christ's first coming, whereas the fall feast and celebration pointed to events surrounding His second coming. Taking these facts together with the date of the the Jewish Day of Atonement falling on October 22, 1844, they fixed upon this time when Christ would come to execute judgment and purge the earth of sin. God also took them to the parable of the 10 virgins in Matthew 25 where He calls for His people to go forth prepared to meet the bridegroom. As they studied the parable, they noticed that the bridegroom tarried and all of the virgins fell asleep while their lamps continued to burn. At midnight, the virgins were awaken by the cry "Behold, the bridegroom cometh; go ye out to meet Him" (Matt 25:6). Although all the virgins arose and trimmed their lamps, only those who had taken extra oil were prepared for the tarrying, and, at His coming "they that were ready went in with Him to the marriage" (Matt 25:10). This tarrying seem to explain why Christ did not come in the spring of 1844, and the message of the coming of the bridegroom went forth like and overwhelming landslide in the summer and autumn of 1844. As the time drew near, the churches began to withdraw their support from the preaching of Christ's soon return, and even sought to prevent their parishioners from going elsewhere to hear the message. As a result, about 50000 believers withdrew from these churches, and immediately the media, both secular and religious, came forth with publications decrying, that there was a great spiritual declension in the churches. Thus, the 2nd angels message of Rev 14:8 sounded as the condition of those steeped in error, falsehood, tradition, and customs, who were spiritually indifferent and caught up in the industrial revolution, was made manifest. Thereafter, the churches began to retreat back to spiritual Babylon. The coming of the bridegroom at midnight identifies the coming associated with the midnight watch, and **we entered the watch of the cockcrowing October 22, 1844**. In this transition, Christ passed from the holy to the most holy place of the heavenly sanctuary to carry out His final work of atonement which involves a work of examination and judgment to determine those who shall be the subjects of His everlasting kingdom. **We are now living in the Antitypical Day of Atonement when all who have ever professed faith in Christ and have entered the service of God will be weighed in the balances of the sanctuary to determine who, by their faith and loyalty to God, shall be found worthy of eternal life with the Lord. It is the time when the 3rd angel's message of Rev14:9-12 is to be proclaimed to prepare a people for that coming that is associated with the cockcrowing.**

B. Since the last destruction of the earthly sanctuary was in AD 70, the cleansing to take place at the termination of the 2300 year prophecy in 1844 could only have reference to the heavenly sanctuary which was

the pattern for the earthly. Christ is now clothed in His high priestly garments and carrying forward His final work of atonement during the Antitypical Day of Atonement.
1. **Christ is represented as having deep love and tender regard for His people, carrying our interest and concerns upon His heart** (typified by the breastplate of judgment) and **as bearing our burdens upon His shoulders** (typified by the onyx stones).
2. In this sin offering, **He is not** represented **as a lamb** - dumb and not uttering His voice when led to the slaughter - **but as a goat - a protector and defender of His flock.**

C. **With His own blood He makes atonement** for the most holy place, the holy place, the golden altar, and for all who have professed faith in Him who have ignorantly broken the law of God and who have confessed and repented of their sins - **to cleanse us that we may be clean of all of our sins, to purge our conscience from dead works, that we may be perfect** (Lev 16:30; Heb 9:13, 14; 7:11; 6:1-3).

"Those living upon the earth when the intercession of Christ shall cease in the sanctuary above are to stand in the sight of a Holy God without a mediator. Their robes must be spotless, their characters must be purified from sin by the blood of sprinkling. Through the grace of God and their own diligent effort they must to be conquerors in the battle with evil. While the investigative judgment is going forward in heaven, while the sins of penitent believers are being removed from the sanctuary, there is to be a special work of purification, of putting away of sin, among God's people upon the earth. This work is more clearly presented in the messages of Rev 14." GC page 425

D. **And the third angel of Rev 14:9-12 begin to sound** with the most fearful warning, the most dreadful threatening ever communicated unto mankind: **"If any man worship the beast and his image, and receive his mark in his forehead, or in his hand, the same shall drink of the wine of the wrath of God, which is poured out without mixture into the cup of His indignation."** This message is designed to put the children of God upon their guard, by showing them the hour of temptation and anguish that is before them. The 3rd angel closes his message thus: **"Hear is the patience of the saints: Here are they that keep the commandments of God, and have the faith of Jesus.**

As he repeated these words, he pointed to the Heavenly Sanctuary. **The minds of all who embrace this message are directed to the Most Holy Place where Jesus stands before the the ark, making His final intercession for all those for whom mercy still lingers, and for those who have ignorantly broken the law of God.** ER page 254

1. As the people anciently fasted and afflicted their souls that their minds might be clear to follow their high priest in this closing work of atonement, so are those living during this Antitypical Day of Atonement to do. **The antitype of that fast is the health reform message that God has given His people to help fit them for the coming of the Lord.** CDF page 97
2. **Those who proclaim the 3rd Angels Message are to teach health reform.** It is a subject that we must understand **to be prepared for the events that are close upon us, and it is to have a prominent place.**" CDF page 109

E. The high priest, going out into the court after making an end of reconciling the two apartments, figuratively bears all the confessed sins of Israel out of the tabernacle and confesses them upon the head of the scapegoat. This represents Christ at His 2nd Advent to the earth when He will confess the sins of all the redeemed upon the head of Satan (Azazal), the great originator and instigator of sin. As the wicked perish in the brightness of Christ's coming, and the righteous are caught up forever to be with the Lord, **Satan will be bound to a now desolate and uninhabited earth, nevermore to harass and tempt God's people. Bearing the guilt of all the sins that he has caused God's people to commit, Satan will be confined to the earth for a thousand years, awaiting the final execution of judgment in which he, the fallen angels, and all the wicked of the earth shall perish in the consuming fire of God's glory** (Malachi 4:1-3; Heb 12:29; Isa 33:14, 15). "Thus the great plan of redemption will reach its accomplishment in the final eradication of sin and in the deliverance of all who have been willing to renounce evil" (GC page 486).

HOW IMPORTANT IS IT THAT WE UNDERSTAND THAT "THY WAY O GOD IS IN THE SANCTUARY"? ER page 55-56; GC page 430-431; Psalms 77:13

Chapter XVI

DANIEL 9

WHEN GOD'S FACE SHINES UPON THE SANCTUARY THE SHADOW MEETS THE SUBSTANCE THAT CAST THE SHADOW

I. **In Humility Before the Omniscient God, Understanding is Established.**
   A. In the first year that Darius the Mede sat upon the throne of universal empires, commencing in 538BC, the year that his nephew Cyrus led the combine armies of the Medes & Persians to lay siege to and overthrow Babylon, Daniel set his mind to study the prophecies of Jeremiah that he might ascertain the years that Jerusalem was to remain in ruins, the time when God would turn back the captivity of His people, and when the restoration of all things would commence. Jer 25:11, 13, 29:10-14
      1. Then did the prophet himself began to fulfill the very prophecies that confirmed his understanding of the 70 years of Jerusalem's desolation, and he humbled himself before the Lord and sought Him with prayer and supplication, with fasting and sackcloth and ashes. Jer 29:10-14, Dan 9:3 In verses 5 & 6 **Daniel identified himself with the sins, the iniquity, the wickedness of a chosen but rebellious people,** though no such evil was found in him.

In verses 7 to 14 **the prophet vindicates the actions of God in His dealings with His people: Extolling the Lord for His righteousness and mercies; and pointing back to the Mosaic record that forewarned God's people of the judgments that would follow sin and rebellion.** In verses 15 and 16 **the prophet points to the great glory and renown that God had gotten for Himself** in His mighty deliverance of Israel from Egyptian bondage that was now held in reproach by the heathen nations. **Then did Daniel plead with God to turn away His anger, to turn back the captivity of His people for His name's sake and for His honor, that He might again be glorified before the heathen.**

II. **Gabriel, Make This Man to Understand the Vision.** Dan 8:16
   A. **Finally, Daniels mind fixed upon that which was the burden of his soul,** that which so troubled him that he was smitten with sickness and astonished at the vision, but did not understand it.
   "Now therefore, O God, hear the prayer of thy servants, and his supplication, and cause Thy face to shine upon Thy sanctuary that is desolate, for the Lord's sake" (Dan 9:17).
   What is this long duration of time, 2300 years, in which paganism and the papacy are to trample under foot both the sanctuary and those who worship therein? **Then did Gabriel fly swiftly to Daniel's side while he was yet in prayer,** to give him skill and understanding, to show him the things of his petition, to reveal to him how greatly beloved he is. Therefore , said Gabriel, **"understand the matter, and consider the vision."** Dan 9:17-23
       1. **Which vision, Lord?** The only vision that God gave to Daniel in which Gabriel was commissioned to make him to understand it. In the vision of Dan 2, first given to Nebuchadnezzar, then to Daniel with the vision's interpretation, Gabriel did not appear.
       In the first of a series of visions that God gave to Daniel, in chap.7, which portrays the rise and fall of universal empires symbolized as beast of prey rising out of the wind-tossed sea, again Gabriel did not appear. Neither did the prophet conclude that he failed to understand either of these visions. Though his cogitation about the vision of chapter 7 much troubled him, he understood and

kept the matter in his heart. Thus we are brought to the vision of chapter 8. In this chapter the angel
Gabriel appears to Daniel with the commissioned to make him to understand the vision regarding the activity of the ram, the he goat, and the little horn - summed up as paganism and the papacy trampling under foot both the sanctuary and those who worship therein. It was when Gabriel began to answer the question, "How long the vision …?" And then declared
"Unto two thousand and three hundred days; then shall the sanctuary be cleansed ," that Daniel fainted, fell sick, and "was astonished at the vision, but none understood it." Therefore, Gabriel had to cease his communications. In chapter 9, Gabriel returns to complete the work that he started in chapter 8, to "**make this man to understand the vision**" (Dan 8:16, 9:22, 23).

III. **The Messiah, The Christ, and the 70 weeks or 490 day/year Prophecy!**
   A. The angel Gabriel begins where he left off - dealing with time.
   "The vision" of the (2300) evenings and mornings "which was told is true …. for it shall be for many days" (Dan 2:26). Gabriel then declares that 70 weeks of the 2300 days/years prophecy are determined upon the Jews and Jerusalem. In other words **490 years of the 2300 years are specifically allotted to the Jews to "finish the transgression, to make an end of sins, to make reconciliation for iniquity, to bring in everlasting righteousness, to seal up the vision and prophecy, and to anoint the most holy."** Dan 8:26, 9:24
      1. How, pray tell, could sinful, mortal men ever fulfill so high, holy, and exalted requirements of God? **Only in receiving Christ by faith as a personal Savior, that we might appropriate unto ourselves the merits of His holy life and sacrificial death, His triumphant resurrection and glorious ascension, and His triumphal entry into the Heavenly Sanctuary where He ministers as our Great High Priest.** **Christ** finished the transgression; **Christ** made an end of sins; **Christ** made reconciliation for iniquity; **Christ** brought in everlasting righteousness; **Christ** sealed up the vision and the prophecy as in Him type met antitype, and the shadow met the substance that cast the shadow; and **Christ** ascended to anoint the Most Holy- the Heavenly Sanctuary where He ministers

as our Great High Priest. **Only by receiving Jesus as their Savior, the long looked for Messiah - the Christ - the Anointed One, would the Jews remain God's chosen people, the depositaries of His Holy Law, the agents for the spreading of the gospel.** Thus, even before examining the 70 week prophecy, we ascertain that it must bring us to the first Advent of our Lord and Savior..

B. Having cut out 490 years from the 2300 years and told what must be accomplished by the end thereof, Gabriel next gives the starting point for the reckoning of the prophetic periods.

   1. **From the going forth** of the commandment to restore and to build Jerusalem (Dan 9:25). Notice: an ancient monarch's reigns was reckoned from fall to fall. **Ezra 6:14 reveals that it would require the decree of three kings of Persia to initiate, reaffirm, and finalize the decree according to the commandment of God.**

   Cyrus decree of 536BC, coming 70 years after the Jews went into Babylonian captivity, dealt primarily with the building of the temple, which was the earthly sanctuary and house of the Lord God of heaven (Ezra 1:1-4).

   Darius Hystaspes's decree of 521/520BC reaffirmed and called for the expeditious prosecution of the decree of Cyrus heretofore hindered by the Samaritans. Darius' decree called for the destruction of anyone who would alter the king's word, and that, "the God that that hath caused his name to dwell there destroy all kings and people, that shall put their hand to alter or destroy this house of God which is at Jerusalem" (Ezra 6:11, 12). "And the elders of the Jews builded, and they prospered through the prophesying of Haggai the prophet and Zechariah the son of Iddo. And they builded, and finished it according to the of command of the God of Israel, and …. of Cyrus, and Darius, and Artaxerxes king of Persia. And this house was finished on the 3rd day of the month Adar (Sept), which was in the 6th year of the reign of Darius the king" in 516/515 BC (Ezra 6:14, 15).

   The original decree of Artaxerxes Longimanus, written not in Hebrew, as is the rest of the book of Ezra, but in the official Chaldaic, or Eastern Aramaic, is preserved in Ezra 7. This decree specified: "Whatsoever is commanded by the God of heaven, let it be diligently done for the house of the God of heaven" (Ezra 7:23).

It added that it shall be unlawful "to impose toll, tribute, or custom" on ministers of the house of God. The decree directed Ezra, after the wisdom of his God, to "set magistrates and judges" (Ezra 7:25). Thus. this final decree made provision for the religious, civil, and judicial government of Jerusalem. Artaxerxes accession year was from Dec 465/Jan 464 to the fall of 464. The 1st year of his reign was from Dec 464/Jan 463 - fall 463. Ezra declares that he made preparation to return the 1st day of 1st month Nisan (Oct) and departed for Jerusalem the 12th day. The decree making provision for the return of any exiles was made in the fall 457 according to the civil year reckoning of the year. Ezra and the returning exiles arrived in Jerusalem on the 1st day of the 5th month Ab (Feb), in the spring of 456.

Zerubbabel's and Joshua's primary task in the return of the 1st exiles was to build the house of the Lord God, the earthly sanctuary. 79 years later Ezra's primary task was to build up the people of Israel, teaching them God's statutes and judgments, and the history of His dealings with Israel. Nehemiah's primary task in coming to Jerusalem 13 years after Ezra as the appointed governor by king Artaxerxes, was to build the walls and gates of Jerusalem, a defense against surrounding enemies.

Ezra 1:1-4, 6:1-12, 14, Dan 9:25, Ezra 7:6-19, 8:31, 7:11-26

C. **Next, Gabriel breaks up the 490 years into junctures of time specifying what event was to be accomplished by the end of each time period.**
  1. **At the end of 7 weeks - 49 days/years - Jerusalem was to be rebuilt.** History bears witness to the fact that Jerusalem was rebuilt by the year 408BC from the starting point of 457BC. Dan 9:25
  2. **At the end of 62 weeks - 434 days/years from 408BC, the Messiah the Prince was to appear.** The Messiah/Christ means the Anointed One, He who would be the Savior of mankind. 434 years from fall of 408BC brings us to **the fall of AD 27,** the time when **Jesus of Nazareth was anointed by God the Father and the Holy Spirit** to enter upon His ministry. Mark 1:9-12 After His victory gained in the wilderness of temptation over Satan, Jesus came preaching the gospel saying **"The time is fulfilled, and the kingdom of God is at hand."** What time, Lord? **The time of Daniels prophecy**

indicating when the Messiah, the Christ, the Anointed One of God, would appear. Acts 10:38, Dan 9:25

D. Jesus was to "confirm the covenant with many for one week: And in the midst of the week He shall cause the sacrifice and oblation to cease." The first 7 weeks brought us to the restoration of Jerusalem. The next 62 weeks brought us to the Messiah - to the baptism and anointing of Jesus to began His ministry. This leaves only 1 week of the 70 weeks prophecy. **Jesus Himself confirmed the covenant with the Jews for the 1st three and a half years, then He was crucified in the spring of AD 31. Before** His crucifixion, Christ gave instruction to His disciples whom He had called, trained, mentored, and sent forth to, "Go not in the way of the Gentiles, and into any city of the Samaritans enter ye not: but go rather to the lost sheep of the house of Israel" (Matt 10:5, 6). The disciples continued to do this for the remaining 3.5 years until Stephen was stoned in the fall of AD 34. At this time the disciples were scattered abroad and they took the gospel to the Gentiles as well as to Israel. With the termination of the 70 week prophecy, the Jews sealed their rejection of Christ as foretold by the prophet Daniel (Dan 9:24), and spiritual Israel took the place of literal Israel as God's agents for the spreading of the gospel (Dan 9: 26, 27; Luke 19:42-44; Matt 23:37-39; Gal 3:7-10; Rom 10:1-13).

As we come to the end of Dan 9 it is clear that Gabriel has not revealed all that is to be understood about the vision of the 2300 evenings and mornings.

IV. **The 2300 Day Prophecy culminates with events transpiring during the the Antitypical Day of Atonement and surrounding the 2nd advent of Christ** (GC Chapters 23, 24, & 28).

    A. As surely as the 490 year prophecy brought us to events surrounding Christ's 1st Advent, so surely does the 2300 years bring us to events surrounding His 2nd Advent.

        1. **"Then shall the sanctuary be cleansed"** The 490 year prophecy brought us to the fall of AD 34. Subtracting 490 from 2300 leaves 1810 years of the prophecy which reach to the fall of 1844.

        The cleansing of the sanctuary occurred the 10th day of the 7th month - called the Day of Atonement - and it involved the removal or blotting out of the sins that had accumulated during the daily ministry. This was to cleanse the sanctuary and all Israel whose sins had gone before in confession and repentance for the forgiveness of sins. The last earthly sanctuary of God was destroyed by Rome in AD 70 (Luke 19:41-44; Matt 23:37). Therefore, this cleansing could only have reference to the great original sanctuary in heaven, which was the pattern for the earthly, and **the termination of the 2300 years brought us to the Antitypical Day of Atonement when Christ commences His final work of atonement** in behalf of humanity. However, before this work of blotting out of sins can be accomplished, there must be an examination of the record books to determine who, through repentance of sin and faith in Christ, are entitled to the benefits of His final work of Atonement and have their names eternally enshrined in the book of life. Thus the cleansing of the sanctuary involves a work of investigation and judgment. This we saw in Daniel 7 when the Ancient of days took His seat as the presiding official in the judgment. When Christ ceases this ministry, the destiny of every human soul will have been decided, and He will have determined those who shall be the subjects of His everlasting kingdom; and the solemn words of Rev 22:11, 12 will be uttered. Lev 23:26-30

B. **The 2300 year prophecy may be said to specify a definite time period at the end of which Christ's final work of atonement in an Investigative Judgment commenced.** It must also be recognized that the prophecy implies an indefinite period of time during which the investigative judgement goes forward. **At the end of the definite time period,** each the following scriptures were fulfilled: GC 424-427

  1. **"The Ancient of Days did sit .... the judgment was set,** and the books were open ...... and behold, one like the Son of Man ... came to the Ancient of days ...... And there was given Him dominion, and glory, and a kingdom." Dan 7:9, 10, 13, 14
  2. **"Then shall the sanctuary be cleansed."** Dan 8:14
  3. **"The Lord, whom ye seek, shall come suddenly to His temple ...... and He shall sit as a refiner and purifier** ..... and He shall purify the sons of Levi .... that they may offer unto the Lord an offering in righteousness. Malachi 3:1-3

4. "And at midnight there was a cry made, **Behold the Bridegroom cometh;** go ye out to meet Him. **And they that were ready went in with Him to the marriage**" (Matt 25: 6, 10)
5. "And **The 3rd Angel followed** them, **saying** with a loud voice, **If any man worship the beast and his image, and receive his mark in his forehead, or in his hand: The same shall drink of the wrath of God, which is poured out without mixture into the cup of His indignation** .... Here is the patience of the saints: Here are they that keep the commandments of God, and the faith Jesus" (Rev 14:9-12).

C. **Since 10-22-1844 we have been in the indefinite time period.** No time prophecy extends beyond this date. No message to the people of God based in definite time extends beyond October 22, 1844. The events to take place beyond this date with no specified duration of time are:

1. **The Work of the Investigative Judgment** begun October 22, 1844 is now going forward (Dan 7:9-14; Mal 3:1-6; Rev 14:7)
2. **The Cleansing of the Sanctuary** begun October 22, 1844 is now going forward (Dan 8:14; Mal 3:1-6).
3. **The invitation to the marriage of the Bridegroom** is now going forward before the door is shut.
4. **The purifying of God's remnant people** is now going forward
5. **The 3rd angels message of warning** is now being given to the world to prepare the people for Christ's 2nd Coming. The 1st angels messages was proclaimed from the fall of 1833 to the fall of 1844, and the message of the 2nd angel from the summer to the fall of 1844: The first 2 messages prepared the way for the work of the 3rd angel of Rev 14 whose work commenced October 22, 1844. In order to understand and be actively engaged in the work of the 3rd angel we must have a clear understanding of the work of the first 2 angels. Hence all 3 messages are being proclaimed during this period of the 3rd angel (Rev 14:6-12).

> **"** Since 10-22-1844 we have been in the indefinite time period. No time prophecy extends beyond this date. **"**

D. Those who are said to follow Christ into the heavenly sanctuary and worship Him therein; those who seek Him in His temple and are purged when He sits as a refiner; those who follow Him when He comes with the clouds of heaven ….. to the Ancient of Days and judgment; those who are ready to go in with Him to the marriage - these are they who receive and become agents of God to proclaim the 3 angel's messages of warning. These are the ones who are said to exhibit the patience of the saints, who keep the commandments of God and the faith of Jesus (Rev 14:12).

Chapter XVII

DANIEL 10 & 11 PART 1

PRIMARY KINGS OF PERSIA & GREECE TO THE KING OF THE NORTH & THE SOUTH

I. A Vision Understood
   A. In the 3rd year of Cyrus, the sovereign ruler over the universal world empire, Daniel speaks of understanding the vision of the 2300 years, which began in Dan 8, was expounded upon in Dan 9, and continued here in Daniel 10:1-4.
   B. Daniel sees a vision of Christ gloriously revealed before him. Compare Dan 10:5-8 with Rev 1:10-17, Ezek 1:24-28, Isa 6:1-5 So holy and sublime is the vision that the prophet loses all strength. Gabriel is sent to Daniel to strengthen him, and to disclose to him the work that he has been doing to urge the kings of Persia to do God's will, and the difficulty that he encountered as Satan opposed him, until Michael, the 1st of the chief Princes, the Son of God, came to his aid. Who is Michael?
      1. The name **"Michael"** means **"He who is like God"**
      2. Jude 9 declares that **Michael is the archangel, the head of the angels.**
      3. The Apostle Paul ascribes the title "archangel" to Christ at His 2nd advent when His voice is heard calling forth those who have died in Him (1 Thes 4:16; John 5:25, 26).

4. **Gabriel** declares that the only one who holds a greater position than he is Michael, whom he describes as Daniel's "Prince." The only heavenly being to whom Daniel or any other human can lay claim to as being their Prince, is Christ - the Prince of peace, the Prince of the covenant (Dan 10:21; Isa 9:6).
C. Gabriel further discloses to Daniel that he is "come to make" him "understand what shall befall" his "people in the latter days: for yet the vision is for many days" (Dan 10:14). Thus, Gabriel came to give Daniel insight into the remaining 1810 years of the 2300 year prophecy, taking him down to the events surrounding Christ's 2nd advent.

II. History of the Persian Empire
A. Gabriel tells Daniel, "now will I return to fight with the prince of Persia: and when I am gone forth, lo, the prince of Grecian shall come" (Dan 10:20).
Darius the Mede is dead and Cyrus now sits upon the throne of the universal empire with Persia gaining the ascendency over Media. "There shall stand up yet 3 kings in Persia; and the 4th shall be far richer than they all" (Dan 11:2), before a new power arises to take the sovereignty of the earth:

1. **Cyrus reigned over the universal empire 536-530 BC**
2. **Cambyses II, called Ahasuerus in Ezra 4:6,** which probably has reference to his Chaldee name - Ahasuems, **reigned 530-522 BC.**

> "There shall stand up yet 3 kings in Persia; and the 4th shall be far richer than they all" (Dan 11:2), before a new power arises to take the sovereignty of the earth

3. **Darius Hystaspes I deposed and killed the false Smerdis** after he reigned in Persia 6 months. He was a magian prince from Media who personated Cyrus's dead son Smerdis. In Ezra 4:7-24, he is called Artaxerxes, the one who passed the decree causing the Jews to cease from building the temple of God.
Darius reigned from 522 to 486BC.
4. **Xerxes I is called Ahasuerus in the book of Esther.** It was during his reign that Satan sought to exterminate all Israelites within the realm of Persia. **He reigned from 486 to 464BC**
5. **Artaxerxes Longimanus I** was used of God to finalize the decree for the rebuilding and restoration of Jerusalem, sending Ezra to

build up the exiles by teaching them God's laws, statutes, and judgments; and Nehemiah 13 years later as governor to oversee the building of the walls and gates of the city of Jerusalem. **He reigned from 464 to 424BC.** Ezra 7 & Nehemiah 2:1-11

"And the 4th" from Cyrus was Xerxes. He "shall be far richer than they all: and by his strength through his riches he shall stir up all against the realm of Grecia" (Dan 11:2). Passing over 9 minor kings of Persia, the prophet introduces Alexander the Great, the mighty king of the Greeks.

III. History of the Grecian Empire. Dan 11:3-15
A. "A mighty king shall stand up, that shall rule with a great dominion, and do according to his will. And when he shall stand up, his kingdom shall be broken, and shall be divided towards the 4 winds of heaven, and not to his posterity, nor according to his dominion which he ruled: For his kingdom shall be plucked up, even for others besides those." Dan 11:3, 4

If we failed in understanding the rise and fall of the Grecian Empire as portrayed in the visions, images, and symbols of:
1. The brass belly and thighs of the metallic image of Dan 2.
2. The leopard like beast with 4 heads and 4 wings of a fowl in Dan 7
3. The he goat with the notable horn between its eyes that was broken, and in whose place there came up 4 notable horns toward the 4 winds of heaven in Dan 8.

The language here is too plain to be misconstrued or misunderstood.

B. In keeping with the principle of enlargement through repetition, the prophecy next introduces greater detail of the history of the Grecian Empire. The 4 divisions into which the empire was divided by the 4 leading generals of Alexander may well be reckoned from Palestine, the central part of the empire.
1. Ptolemy had that area south of Palestine.
2. Lysimachus had that area north of Palestine.
3. Cassandra had that division west of Palestine.
4. Seleucus had that division east of Palestine.

This first division of the empire determined the name that each portion of the territory should ever afterwards be designated. In other words, whatever power at any time should occupy the territory which at first

constituted the north, that power would be designated the king of the north so long as it occupied that territory. We quickly learn that the 4 divisions of Alexander's empire were eventually reduced to 2 divisions, the north and the south:
1. The Egyptian division to the south was strong, but the division to the north was made even stronger by the consolidation of the other 3 divisions into one. The successors to Cassandra were soon conquered by the successors of Lysimachus, who were in turn conquered by those of Seleucus. Thus the north, east, and west were united into one, the Greco-Syriac division, and Seleucus was termed the king of the north in opposition to the king of the south (Dan 11:5). Both were hellenized, but the north was more truly Greek. The south was strongly tinctured with Egyptian ideas of government and religion. The north correspond to the part of the Grecian Empire that carried forward the work of prophecy in the leopard like beast of Dan 7 and the he goat of Dan 8 out of which arose the the little horn.

The Southern Line	The Northern Line
1. Ptolemy I Soter	1. Seleucus I Nicator
2. Ptolemy II Philadelphus	2. Antiochus I Soter
3. Ptolemy III Euregetes	3. Antiochus II Theos
4. Ptolemy IV Philopater	4. Seluecus II Calinicus
5. Ptolemy V Epiphanes	5. Seleucus III Ceraunus
(210 to 180 BC)	6. Antiochus III The Great
	(Magnus, 223-187 BC)

Note: The Ptolemies coexisted as both Egyptian pharaohs and Greek monarchs. They remained completely Greek in their language and traditions.-

C. Following frequent wars between the north and the south, Dan 11:6 portrays a **marriage** between the daughter of Ptolemy Philadelphus - **Berenice, and Antiochus Theos,** who temporarily put away his current wife, Laodice, for the sake of peace. When brought back, Laodice caused Theos to be poisoned and caused Berenice and her infant son to be murdered, and so managed affairs to secure the throne for her eldest son, Calinicus.

D. In Dan 11:7-9 **Berenice's brother, Ptolemy Euergetes,** "a branch out of the same roots as she," raised an immense army and invaded the north to **avenge the death of his sister.** He prevailed and slew Laodice. Yet, hearing of sedition in Egypt that required his return, he plundered the kingdom of Seleucus by taking 40,000 talents of silver and precious vessels, and 2500 images of the gods. But for his recall, Ptolemy would have possessed the whole kingdom of Seleucus.

E. As war ensued, the sons of Calinicus, particularly Antiochus Magnus, recovered Syrian territory that Ptolemy Euergetes had taken. However, in the battle of Raphis, Antiochus was defeated and the "multitude of his army was given into the hand" of the king of the south, Ptolemy Philopater, who was soon advanced to the crown of the south after Antiochus Magnus ascended the throne of the north. Instead of following up his success to possess the whole of the kingdom of Antiochus, Ptolemy Philopater made peace that he might give himself up to feasting and sensuality. The peace lasted 14 years until Ptolemy died from intemperance and debauchery, and was succeeded by his infant son of 5 years old, Ptolemy Epiphanes. Then Antiochus Magnus raised an immense army, greater than the former, and set out against Egypt, expecting an easy victory over the infant king (Dan 11:10-13).

F. In Dan 11:11-14, we see another power asserting itself to protect the infant king of Egypt. Rome, the robbers of the people who exalted themselves to establish the vision, spoke, and the Greco-Syriac division of the empire soon found a change coming over their aspirations. This was in 200BC and was was but one of the first interferences of the Romans in the affairs of Syria and Egypt. Though the north is seen to come against the south with success in verse 15, verse 16 shows another power coming against the north and doing his own will, and none being able to stand before him. Thus, the narrative immediately carries forward to Rome's conquest of Syria in 65BC.

IV. History of the Roman Empire.
A. **"He that cometh against him (the Greco-Syriac North) shall do according to his own will, and none shall stand before him: And he shall stand in the glorious land, which by his hand shall be consumed."** Dan 11:16
   1. This scripture carriers us forward to the activity of Pompey of the Roman Empire and may parallel the depiction of Rome going forth

to new conquest in Dan 8:9 toward the south, the east, and toward the pleasant land. The western horn of the goat - Macedonia, had already been conquered in 168BC (Dan 8:9).

2. The king of the north above is the Syrian division of the Grecian Empire corresponding to the east in Dan 8:9. In 65BC Pompey deprived Antiochus 13, Asiaticus, of his possessions and reduced Syria to a Roman province, and thus waxed toward the east.

3. The Romans became connected with the people of God, the Jews, by an alliance in 161BC. Rome did not conquer Judea and make it a Roman province until 63BC under the exploits of Pompey. Judea is called the pleasant land in Dan 8:9, and is called the glorious land in Dan 11:16. Thus, Rome waxed toward Judea. This scripture further indicates that Rome would hold Judea in its iron grasp till it had utterly consumed it.

4. Egypt was now all that remained of the whole kingdom of Alexander. Verse 17 picks up here in tracing Roman History.

Chapter XVIII

DANIEL 11 PART 2

HISTORY OF THE ROMAN EMPIRE TO THE 1ST ADVENT OF CHRIST

I. History of the Roman Empire
   A. **Verse 16 brought us to the conquest of Syria (65BC) and Judea (63BC) by the Romans.** Rome had previously conquered Macedon and Thrace. Egypt was now all that remained of the whole kingdom of Alexander. Rome now set his face to enter by force into the land of Egypt (DR page 247, Dan 11:16, 17).
   B. Ptolemy XII Auletes died 51BC & the crown went to his eldest surviving daughter, Cleopatra VII, and his elder son, Ptolemy XIII, who was about 10 years old. Because of their youth, they were placed under the guardianship of the Romans, and it was provided that they should marry each other and reign jointly. **The Roman Senate appointed Pompey as the guardian of the young heirs of Egypt** (DR page 247-248).
   C. **Enter Julius Caesar.** A quarrel broke out between Pompey and Caesar that reached its climax in the **famous battle of Pharsalus. Pompey was defeated,** fled into Egypt, and was basely murdered at the instigation of Ptolemy XIII. Caesar, on arriving in Egypt to assume the guardianship of Ptolemy and Cleopatra, found them hostile toward one another and the country in commotion. Requiring that the opposing armies disband, Caesar decreed that the brother and sister should occupy the

throne jointly, according to the will. Yet, he himself was conquered by the seductive beauty of the ambitious queen. Ptolemy's factions fearing the exaltation of Cleopatra, excited jealousy and hostility against Caesar by insinuating that he designed to eventually give Cleopatra sole power. Open sedition followed and war broke out. A decisive battle was fought near the Nile by the fleet of Egypt and Rome resulting in a complete victory for Caesar. Ptolemy was slain. Alexandria and all of Egypt then submitted to the victor. The arrival of about 3000 Jews under Antipater the Idumean to hold the frontier gateway into Egypt, helped to decide the contest, when they allowed the Romans to pass without interruption (DR page 248-251). With this history in mind, verse 17 would read: **Rome (under Caesar) would "set his face to enter with the strength of his whole kingdom" into Egypt, and the Jews would help him. "Thus shall he do:" And Caesar shall take unto himself Cleopatra, the dissolute queen, to be his mistress, but she shall not stand on the side of Rome (after the base murder of Caesar) but shall join herself to Mark Antony, the enemy of Augustus Caesar, and exert her whole power against Rome.** Dan 11:17

D. In verse 18 we see Caesar being drawn away from Egypt to war in Syria and Asia Minor against Pharnaces, the king of the Cimmerian Bosporus, in which Caesar gain an absolute victory. "An account whereof he wrote to a friend of his in these three words:
Veni, vidi, vici! I came, I saw, I conquered" (DR page 264).

E. After the conquest of Asian Minor, **Caesar** defeated the last remaining fragments of Pompey's party. **Returning to Rome, the "fort of his own land," he was made dictator for life. Shortly afterwards, he was murdered by men he had cared for, protected, or spared.**
Thus, in 44 BC, **"he shall stumble and fall, and not be found"** (Dan 11:19).

F. **Verse 20 brings us to the Augustan Age when Rome reached the pinnacle of its greatness and power. Octavius succeeded his uncle, Julius Caesar.** He publicly announced his adoption by Caesar and took his name. He joined with Mark Antony and Lepidus in what was called the triumvirate to avenge the death of Julius Caesar. When firmly established , the senate conferred on him the title of Augustus. Caesar Augustus was definitely a raiser of taxes and was reigning when Christ was born (Luke 2:1). Augustus died in AD 14 at the age of 76, "neither in anger, nor in battle," but peacefully in his bed, at Nola, where he had gone to seek repose and health (DR, pg. 266).

G. **Caesar Augustus was succeeded by Tiberius Caesar, a vile person, whom the citizens never gave the love, respect, and honor of the kingdom due an upright and faithful sovereign.** Tyranny, hypocrisy, debauchery, and uninterrupted intoxication characterized the life of Tiberius to perfection. In verse 22, we learn that Tiberius would meet with a violent death, and that, during his reign, Christ, the Prince of the covenant, would also meet with a violent death, "shall be broken." Tiberius was smothered to death in March 37 AD at the age of 78, and Jesus was crucified in 31 AD (DR, page 266-269).

Thus, we are brought to 3.5 years before the end of the 70 weeks prophecy, to the culminating event surrounding the 1st advent of Christ - His sacrifice on Calvary's cross. The prophet portrayed the secular events of the Roman Empire in revealing the 3 individuals who successively ruled the empire. Verse 23 takes us back in time to the league that Rome made with the surrounding peoples/countries as it expanded its empire (as Egypt did in I-B above). From that point we are taken through a direct line of events to the final triumph of the church and the setting up of God's everlasting kingdom.

Chapter XIX

DANIEL 11 PART 3 ROME & ISRAEL TO THE RISE OF THE PAPACY

I. From the League with Rome to World Prominence and Power.
   A. From the time of the **league**, Rome worked cunningly to enter upon and acquire valuable provinces and rich territory, not by war and conquest, as nations before him had done, but by peaceable means. **The custom was inaugurated by which kings left their kingdoms to the Romans by legacy.** Those who thereby came under the dominion of Rome, were treated with kindness and leniency, and not raped or spoiled by war, retained their possessions. Thus shall Rome **"scatter among them the prey, and spoil, and riches."** vs 23, 24
   B. We are introduced to a prophetic time period when **Rome "shall forecast his devices from (rather than against) the strong holds."** The strong hold was the strong fortress of the seven hilled city of Rome, the seat of the empire, from which he carried out his exploits. A time corresponds to one year or 360 days. Applying prophetic time to this we get 360 years. The starting point for the reckoning of this time is given in vs 25. It was the decisive battle that was fought between Rome and Egypt which fixed the seat of empire at Rome in the hands of one ruler. This was the battle of Actium fought on Sept. 2, 31 BC, between Mark Antony and Augustus Caesar. Question: What led to this battle?

1. Antony, who became the brother in law of Augustus by marrying his sister Octavia, when sent to Egypt on government business fell victim to the charms of Cleopatra. So strong was his passion for her that he finally espoused the interest of Egypt, rejected his wife Octavia to please Cleopatra, and bestowed province after province upon her. He so affronted the Roman people that Augustus had no difficulty leading them to engage in an all out war with Egypt. With Lepidus having been disposed of from the triumvirate, the rule of the empire now lay between Augustus and Antony. Each being determined to possess the whole, they cast the die of war for its possession. **The world was the stake when the two fleets met at the mouth of the Ambracian Gulf, near the city of Actium.** The outcome of the battle was decided when Cleopatra took to flight at the din of the battle when there was no danger, drawing the Egyptian squadron after her. Antony, lost to everything but his blind passion for her, precipitately followed, and thus yielded the victory to Augustus.
   C. Thus, 31BC marks the beginning of the "time" in verse 24. At the end of this period of 360 years we should expect a change to occur in the seat of the empire. In fact, such a change did occur in AD 330 when Constantine the Great established another capital of the empire in Constantinople and moved there.
   D. Verse 26 portrays how that Antony was deserted by his allies and friends, those who fed "of the portion of his meat." Disgusted with Antony's infatuation for Cleopatra his land army and those whom he left in Libya to guard the frontier, declared for Augustus, and, in Egypt, his forces surrendered. In rage and despair, Antony then took his own life. Cleopatra, not long afterward, artfully caused her self to be fatally bitten by an asp, which is another term for Egyptian cobra. Thus, the last of the whole of Alexander's kingdom which stood between Rome and the world was removed.

II. **Then shall Rome return, and return, and return again at the time appointed, and return with intelligence and indignation against the holy covenant.**
   A. **The first return** of verse 28 is when **Augustus** returned from his **successful campaign against Egypt and Antony** with abundant honor and riches.

B. **The second return** mentioned in verse 28 is set at the time beyond which **Rome fixes his attention upon Judaea and Jerusalem,** the people of "the holy covenant, and shall do exploits and return." As a result of God's covenant people rejecting the Holy One of Israel, they locked themselves in the iron grip of Rome until they should be utterly consumed.
  1. Under Vespasian, the Romans invaded Judaea, and took the cities of Galilee, including Chorazin, Bethsaida, and Capernauam where Christ had been rejected. They destroyed the inhabitants, and left nothing but ruin and desolation.
  2. **Titus followed Cestius and besieged Jerusalem for 5 months before the city fell in AD 70.** A terrible famine ensued and the horrors of starvation were so great that "the tender and delicate woman" ate her own children in the straitness of the siege. Deut 28:52-55

  In order to strike terror in the Jews and cause them to surrender, **the Romans daily scourged, tortured, and crucified hundreds of prisoners before the wall of the city.** This dreadful work continued along the Valley of Jehoshaphat and at Calvary until **crosses were erected in so great a number that there was scarcely room to move among them.** And the slaughter within was more dreadful than the spectacle without. **Men and women, old and young, insurgent and priest, those who fought and those who entreated mercy, were hewn down in indiscriminate carnage.** In the siege, **more than a million people perished, and blood flowed down the temple steps like a river.** Not one stone was left upon another that was not thrown down. Thus, we are brought down the stream of time to AD 70 when Rome again returned victoriously from his exploits.

  > " In order to strike terror in the Jews and cause them to surrender, the Romans daily scourged, tortured, and crucified hundreds of prisoners before the wall of the city. "

C. Again Rome is said to return **"at the time appointed" "and come toward the south; but it shall not be as the former, or as the latter"** (Dan 11:29). Victory, honor, riches, and triumph is not to be the outcome of this return. **What time is here represented that signals this next return?**

1. The only time period designated in the delineation of events of this prophecy is the time set forth in verse 24. Thus we are brought down to the year **AD 330 when Constantine the Great established another capital of the empire to the east in Byzantium (later named Constantinople) to appease resentment in the empire between the East (Greek) and West (Latin) over the rule of the empire being in the west.**
   With 2 capitals now competing for resources and attention, and since Constantinople was the hub of all commerce from the Far East and the western world, Rome lost it's prestige and intellectual population as artisans and merchants moved east. Also, Rome was the seat of the Catholic Church, which was competing for influence with the Emperor himself, so the government did it's best to isolate him. This division precipitated the fall of the western half of the empire and brought with it the fall of civilization in Western Europe as barbarians besieged it, ushering in the Dark Ages and leaving the Church as the only beacon of civilization in the West, which is why western science lagged behind eastern science. Thanks to this move by Constantine the Roman Byzantine Empire lasted until 1456 (Dan 11:29).
2. The first part of verse 30 carries us forward to the invasion of the empire by Genseric, king of the Vandals, the height of whose career was the years AD 428-468. Genseric's headquarters was in Africa, and he made repeated piratical sallies, preyed upon Roman commerce, and waged war with the empire from Carthage. Generic became the tyrant of the sea, and before his death, he beheld the final extinction of the empire of the West in AD 476.

D. **The last part of verse 30 points to Rome's return to have "indignation against the holy covenant" and to "have intelligence with them that forsake the holy covenant."**
   1. The Heruli, Goths, and Vandals, who conquered Rome, embraced the Arian faith, and became enemies of the Catholic Church. It was especially for the purpose of exterminating this heresy that Justinian, emperor of the eastern empire, decreed the pope to be the head of the church and the corrector of heretics. **The Bible soon came to be regarded as a dangerous book that should not be read by the common people**, rather, all questions in disputes were to be submitted to the pope. Thus, was indignity heaped

upon the Word of God. The Council of Trent later enacted ten rules regarding prohibited books, ... insidiously framed to check the growing desire for the Word of God. In the 4th rule, the Council prohibits any one from reading the Bible without a license from his bishop or inquisitor; .... founded on a certificate from his confessor that he is in no danger of receiving injury from so doing" (James A. Wylie, The Papacy, pp. 180, 181).

Those who violated these rules were held guilty of mortal sin and did not receive absolution (forgiveness, remission) until they gave up the Bible to their ordinary. Thus the emperor of the eastern empire "had intelligence" and connived with the apostate church of Rome, "them that forsake the holy covenant," for the purpose of promoting heresy (Dan 11:30).

E. Verse 31 bring to view those rulers of the empire who were working in behalf of the papacy against paganism and all other religions.
  1. **The "daily" corresponds to the continual desolation, which is paganism.** So, for the taking away of paganism, we look to the year AD 508, when a mighty crisis had ripened between Catholicism and the pagan influences still existing in the empire. Up to the time of the conversion of Clovis, king of France, in AD 496, the French and other nations of Western Rome were pagan; but following that event, the efforts to convert idolaters to Romanism were crowned with great success. Soon after the year 508, paganism had so declined and Catholicism had so far relatively increased in strength, that the Catholic Church for the first time was able to wage successful warfare against the civil authority of the empire and the church of the east. It is therefore believed that **AD 508 marks the time of the taking away of paganism** (Dan 11:31; 12:11).
  2. **The abomination of desolation, the papacy,** was set up after Justinian's decree of AD 533 giving the holy see of Rome the pre-eminence over the holy see of Constantinople. The edit could not go into effect until the Ostrogoth opposition in the 7 hilled city of Rome was put down. Sending his general Belisarius to accomplish this work, the opposition was put down in AD 538. Therefore **AD 538 marks the setting up of the abomination of desolation and the beginning of the 1260 years of papal supremacy.** Hence the papacy set up her own priestcraft and ministry whose headquarters

was in the imperial 7 hilled city of Rome. Thus the place of Christ's sanctuary was cast down, and **the papacy robbed the world of the knowledge and truth of Christ's priesthood and ministry in the heavenly sanctuary. Popery became the world's despot** endowed with authority over church and state. **Faith was transferred from Christ to the pope of Rome. And the people were taught to look to the pope for the forgiveness of sins and for eternal salvation instead of to Christ** (GC, pp. 55-60).

Chapter XX

DANIEL 11 PART 4

THE 1260 YEARS OF PAPAL SUPREMACY AND THE REFORMATION

I. **The accession of the papacy to the seat of power in the imperial city of Rome in AD 538 marked the beginning of the 1260 year period of papal oppression foretold by the prophets Daniel and John** (Dan 7:21, 25; Rev 13:2, 5; Dan 11: 31-39; GC, pp. 55, 266).

   A. "Persecution opened upon the faithful with greater fury than ever before, and **the world became a vast battlefield**" (GC page 54-55; Dan 8:23-25). "No church within the limits of Romish jurisdiction was long left undisturbed in the enjoyment of freedom of conscience" (GC, pp. 62, 63). **All whom the papacy could not persuade or flatter to acknowledge her supremacy she stretched forth her arms to crush. Corporal punishment, torture, wars, persecutions of all kinds were the methods adopted to compel all to submit to the Roman yoke** (DR chp 7; GC 62-63; Dan 11:38; DA 435-436).

   B. "Such as do wickedly against the covenant" Dan 11:32
      1. Those who compromised their faith for the sake of peace, security, and temporal prosperity, turned away from the true foundation.
      2. Those who thought more of the decree of popes and the decisions of councils then the Word of God.

      These "shall he corrupt by flatteries" (Dan 11:32).

C. **"But the people that do know their God shall be strong, and do exploits."** Dan 11:32
   1. This scripture refers to **those who were undaunted by the opposition of their enemies; those who contended for the faith delivered to the saints; those who regarded the Bible as the only rule of faith and practice and, believing in the perpetuity of the law of God, observed the 7th day Sabbath of the 4th commandment.**
   2. Prominent among these were **the Waldenses, Lollards, Hussites, Albigenses, and Huguenots.**
D. Verse 33 portrays that long period of papal persecution against the faithful mentioned above who were struggling to maintain the truth and instruct others in the way of righteousness. **Many were martyred for their faith who "love not their lives unto death."** They fell by sword, by flame, by captivity, and by spoil. This period, which is described as lasting "many days," is described in other scriptural references as "a time, and times, and half a time" (Dan 12:7; Rev 12:14), as "forty and two months" (Rev 11:2; 13:5), and as "a thousand two hundred and threescore days" (Rev 12:6).

   All of these scriptures refer to the period of papal supremacy (Dan 11:33; GC 54, 55, 266, 267).
E. The Protestant Reformation is the avenue by which the darkness of papal error, falsehood, superstition, tradition, and custom was to be scattered and dispelled. "Now when they shall fall, they shall be holpen (succored by God when feeble and in danger of falling or being overthrown) with a little help; but many shall cleave to them with flatteries. And some of them of understanding shall fall, to try them, and to purge, and to make them white, even to the time of the end; because it is for a time appointed." Dan 11:34, 35
   1. **The Waldenses** witnessed for God centuries before the birth of Luther. Scattered over many lands, **they planted the seed of the reformation that began in the time of Wycliffe (14th Century) and Huss (15th Century), grew broad and deep in the days of Luther (16th Century),** and is **to be carried forward by those willing to suffer all things for The Word of God and the testimony of Jesus** (Rev 1:9; 19:10; AA 11, 12, GC 65, 66, 266, 267).

2. When Martin Luther was forbidden to appear before the Diet of Spires in 1529, the Christian Princes of Germany lodged their protest against the atrocities of Rome. **Their protest gave to the reformed church the name "Protestant." The principles contained in this celebrated protest constitutes the essence of the Protestant Reformation:**
It opposes two abuses of man in matters of faith: The first is the intrusion of the state or civil magistrate, and the second is the arbitrary authority of the church. **Protestantism sets the power of conscience above the state/magistrate, and the authority of the Word of God above the visible church.** In the first, it rejects the civil power in divine things, saying, **"We should obey God rather than man."** Then, it goes further in laying down the principle that **all human teachings should be subordinate to the Oracles of God. Thus, it struck a death blow to the principle by which Rome operates: Claiming the right to coerce conscience and forbid free inquiry!** The same unswerving adherence to the Word of God manifested at that crisis of the Reformation is **the only hope of reform today** (Acts 4:18-20; 5:27-32, 33-42; GC Chp 11 - 197-205).
3. The time appointed brought to view in verse 35 must refer to the many days of the 1260 years of papal supremacy, which ended February 1798. Since that time appointed is associated with the time of the end in the same verse we conclude that **the world entered the time of the end in 1798 when the papal supremacy ended.** Although Matt 24:21, 22 portrays this period of tribulation that was to come upon the church as largely ceasing before the expiration of the time, the spirit of persecution would not be destroyed. Wherever Roman Catholicism still bore sovereign sway over the civil powers, persecution would continue (GC 356).

II. Who is this king suddenly introduced in verse 36 , **doing according to his will, exalting and magnifying himself above every god, and speaking marvelous things against the God of gods, and prospering till the indignation be accomplished"**?
   A. The last power introduced as bearing sovereign sway over the world was the papacy. And the activity of this power was, for "many days," against those who know their God. These "many days," were to reach

to the time of the end. **Inasmuch as verse 36 does not bring us to the time of the end, this king can only be the papacy.**

Upon reaching the time of the end, the indignation will be accomplished.

B. **The Apostle Paul warned the Christians of his day that a great apostasy would occur in the church before the day of Christ return:** "Let no man deceive you by any means; for that day shall not come, except there come a falling away first, **and that man of sin be revealed, the son of perdition; who opposeth and exalteth himself above all that is called God, or that is worshiped; so that he as god sitteth in the temple of God, showing that he is god.**" The outworking of this power is called the mystery of iniquity, whose coming is after the working of Satan with all power and signs and lying wonders. "And with all deceivableness of unrighteousness in them that perish; because they received not the love of truth, that they might be saved." 2 Thes 2:1-12, GC 356

> "The Apostle Paul warned the Christians of his day that a great apostasy would occur in the church before the day of Christ return"

C. **John describes the speaking of this kingly power:** "And there was given him a mouth speaking great things and blasphemies; and power was given unto him to continue 42 months. And he opened his mouth in blasphemy against God, to blaspheme His name, and His tabernacle, and them that dwell in heaven.** And it was given unto him to make war with the saints, and to overcome them: And power was given him over all kindreds, and tongues, and nations" (Rev 13:5-7). Yet, his power is to be broken, for "he that leadeth into captivity shall go into captivity; he that killeth with the sword must be killed with the sword" (Rev 13:10)

Clearly, the same kingly power identified in part II - A, B, and C above is described in Dan 11:36-39.

D. That this king is described as having no regard for the desire of women might lead one to think that the leaders of this kingdom practiced celibacy. However, in keeping with the kingdom's Babylonian roots, just as the vestal virgins of Babylonian sun worship were shut up in a house for women, so the papal system inculcates women in the sisterhood of nuns. In ancient times, vestal virgins, being married to the sun god, were required to minister to the passions, the lust, the sexual desires of those in the priesthood. Likewise, in the papal system, women have been shut up in a nunnery, cut off from all family ties, and often required to serve without question in a similar capacity a supposedly celibate priesthood (Dan 11:37).

E. In the beginning of this study we saw the god of forces employed by this king with his accession to the seat of power in the imperial city of Rome, a god whom his fathers knew not (Dan 11:38, 39).

1. The Papacy emerged from the early Christian Church following about 249 years of pagan persecution from the time of Nero to Constantine, followed by another 225 years of compromise and union between half converted pagans and apostate christians. Thus, her fathers were the apostles, who were chosen, called, trained, mentored, ordained, and sent forth by Christ Himself. **But, God never compels the obedience of man. He leaves all free to choose whom they will serve** (Josh 24:14, 15).

    Therefore, honoring the god of forces was indeed honoring a strange god, considering its origin.

    "There can be no more conclusive evidence that we posses the spirit of Satan than the disposition to hurt or destroy those who do not appreciate our work, or who act contrary to our ideas (DA page 487).

F. This carries us back to the description of the Apostle Paul of the mystery of iniquity - created being seeking to make himself god. That this king increased in glory and divided the land for gain is borne out in history. Daniel tells us that **"his power shall be mighty, but not by his own power: And he shall destroy wonderfully, and shall prosper, and shall practice, and shall destroy the mighty and holy people, and through his policy he shall cause craft to prosper in his hand; and he shall magnify himself in his heart, and by peace shall destroy many: He shall stand up against the Prince of princes (Christ);** but he shall be broken without hands." Dan 8:24, 25, Rev 13:2, 3

III. **Verse 40 brings us to the time of the end - the time when the indignation shall be accomplished, the time when the power of this king is to be broken, the time when the papal supremacy shall end - February 1798.** Before proceeding to interpret the rest of Dan 11 we must recognize that a change has occurred in the Bible reckoning of who now constitutes the chosen people of God. This change or transition demands that the literal, national, local things pertaining to Israel and her enemies be given a spiritual, world wide, international application to the church and her enemies at this time of the end.

Chapter XXI

DANIEL 11 PART 5

SPIRITUAL BABYLON VS ATHEISM, THE FINAL CONFLICT BETWEEN THE KING OF THE NORTH & THE KING OF THE SOUTH

I. That Dan 11:40 brings us to the time of the end is clearly stated. At this time, the papal power is to be broken, as another power comes against her. **To interpret what follows, we must recognize that a transition has occurred which demands that the prophecies that follow be interpreted spiritually rather than literally.** A few points will suffice to establish this.
   A. Jesus told the woman at the well **"Ye worship ye know not what: we know what we worship: for salvation is of the Jews. But the hour cometh, and now is, when the true worshipers shall worship the Father in spirit and in truth: For the Father seeketh such to worship Him."** John 4:22-24

Then, after pronouncing woes upon the scribes and Pharisees, Jesus exclaimed, "O Jerusalem, Jerusalem, thou that killest the prophets, and stonest them which are sent unto you, how often would I have gathered thy children together, even as a hen gathers her chickens under her wings, and ye would not! **Behold, your house is left unto you**

desolate" (Matt 23:37, 38). Thus did Christ point to the end to which the nation was hastening, the destruction of Jerusalem in AD 70. Yet, 3.5 years beyond the crucifixion, they might repent and receive Christ as their personal Savior, and remain God's agents for the spreading of the gospel.

1. With the stoning of Stephen in the fall of AD 34, the 70 week prophetic time allotted unto literal Israel expired (Dan 9:24), and the work of the gospel passed from literal Israel to spiritual Israel, the Christian church (Dan 9:24; Rom 2:28, 29; 9:4-8; Ga 3:7-9; 4:22-31; 5:1).
2. **Was Jesus' statement that salvation is of the Jews still true?**
   Rom 2:28, 29, 9:4-8, Ga 3:6-14, 26-29, 5:1-6, 1Cor 15:42-46
   In these texts, God reveals the true meaning of what it means to be a Jew, reasoning not from literal but from spiritual principles.

B. In lesson III, we saw that, after the Flood, Satan developed a counterfeit system of religion in ancient Babylon to war against the religion of Christ: Paganism, based in the pseudo science of astrology, called the wisdom of the Chaldean (Babylonians). In all pagan philosophies, the doctrine of immortality of the soul is the foundation and center of their whole belief and worship. **Babylonian Mysticism teaches that man is a microcosm, a miniature universe, the ruler of nature, capable of spiritually expanding himself to become god.** It embraces the entire realm of the occult. This counterfeit system has a promised messiah, a form of baptism, a spiritual rebirth, a confession of sins, a communion, and a promise of immortality. Hence, we should expect a spiritual counterpart of this principle agent of Satan used to war against Israel to emerge when literal Israel gives place to spiritual Israel, the Christian Church.

> *Babylonian Mysticism teaches that man is a microcosm, a miniature universe, the ruler of nature, capable of spiritually expanding himself to become god.*

When Rome conquered the Grecian Empire it was as pagan as the 3 universal empires that preceded it, and it embarked upon a political campaign to rule the world. Literally carrying forward all the teachings of Babylonian mysticism, **Rome was called the New Babylon. However, Pagan Rome was to undergo a transition and cloak its pagan sun worship in the** garments of Christianity and present her leader, the pope, whose office and authority is called the papacy, as the vicegerent of God. **Still Rome,** but afterwards to be known as **Spiritual Babylon** in its new form, **Papal Rome.** No longer claiming to be a pagan nation among pagan nations, **she claims to be 'the religion of Christ that has ascended the political seat, power, and authority of the Roman Empire, having sovereign dominion over all churches and nations. Therefore, she has set out to make all peoples, nations, and tongues Catholic. She thereby gains control of the minds and the wealth of the people and the economic, political, and military machinery of the nations.** She claims to be what she is not by nature, practice, or spirit: **Not just a Christian church, but the Christian church, having the right to compel men to accept her faith or have no faith at all. She therefore does not recognize that which distinguishes man from the brute beast** - humanity's free moral agency or liberty of conscience - **the power to make conscientious choices between alternatives, which is a God given endowment that, in matters of conscious, no other person, entity, power, or institution has the right to violate** (GC chap 2 & Rev 13:1-8). **God** alone has jurisdiction over this endowment, and He **operates to preserve not violate the liberty of conscious of all free moral beings.**

C. During the 1260 years of papal supremacy, the papacy made manifest its true character and spirit, and the world learned a lesson that future generations would soon forget. She revealed her leader to be the "man of sin," "the son of perdition," who is ready to destroy, and eliminate all who dissent from her claims. **Pagan in spirit, nature, and practice, she acknowledges no power or authority above her own.** The knowledge that a spiritual warfare is taking place requires a discernment that looks beyond and beneath the mere profession of Christianity. **Spiritual principles must now be employed to discern the nature and the end to which this war is tending.** 2Thes 2:1-9, 1Cor 15:46

II. In Dan 11:15, 16 Rome is seen acting in behalf of Egypt - the king of the south, and subsequently conquers the Greco-Syriac division of the Grecian Empire - the king of the north, in 65 BC. Rome then becomes the king of the north. In verse 25 we see the battle fought between Caesar Augustus representing Rome as the king of the north, and Mark Antony who is united with Cleopatra and Egypt as the king of the south. Caesar Augustus emerges the victor in this war, and he ascends the throne of universal sovereignty of the world in 31 BC, as the last remaining vestige of the Grecian empire is removed. **By the time we get to verse 40 where the king of the south is seen to push at the king of the north, we have transitioned from the literal to the spiritual interpretation of human events.**

What is the true heart of Egyptian ideas & the spirit of her religion?

A. From the first division of Alexander's Empire after his death, the southern division, though Hellenized like the north, was strongly impregnated with Egyptian ideas of government and religion. **Though pagan in nature, practice, and religion, we see in Pharaoh the true spirit and ideology of Egypt.** When confronted by God's servant Moses with the words "Thus saith the Lord God of Israel, let My people go," Pharaoh responded, **"Who is the Lord, that I should obey His voice to let Israel go?" This question is the epitome of disbelief in the existence of the sovereign God.** Pharaoh's question was not to learn about this God, but **to discount His existence. This is the very spirit of atheism.**

B. **What effect did the papacy have in spreading its influence?**

"In the 16th century the Reformation, presenting an open Bible to the people, had sought admission into all the countries of Europe." Some nations welcomed it with gladness. "In other lands the papacy succeeded to a great extent, in preventing its entrance; and the light of Bible knowledge, with its elevating influences, was almost wholly excluded. In one country, though the light found entrance, it was not comprehended by the darkness" (GC, chp 15, page 265). **France stands on record as having wholly thrown the weight of empire on the side of the papacy, and having thrust out the truth of Heaven, descended into the dark abyss of infidelity. Atheism emerged to trample the Law of God underfoot and throw off all moral restraint, and licentiousness became the prevailing characteristics of the nation. France then** proceeded to do what no modern nation had ever done before. **By the action of the highest authority of the nation, the legislative assembly decreed that there was no God.** The institutions of the Bible were abolished, Bibles were publicly burned in the streets, and idolatry soon followed in the institution of the Goddess of Reason GC 269-275 **"Rome had misrepresented the character of God and perverted His requirements, and now men rejected both the Bible and its Author"**

(GC, pg 281). "**It was popery that had begun the work which atheism was completing**" (GC, pg 276). "Unhappy France reaped in blood the harvest she had sown" (pg 282). "Where France, under the influence of Romanism, had set up the 1st stake at the opening of the Reformation, there the Revolution set up it's 1st guillotine. On the very spot where the 1st martyrs to the Protestant faith were burned in the 16th century, the 1st victims were guillotined in the 18th." **The war against the Bible inaugurated an era which stands in the world's history as the Reign of Terror**" (pg 282). "The scaffolds ran red with the blood of priests. The galleys and prisons, once crowded with Huguenots, were now filled with their persecutors" (pg 283). "No one was secure. .... Violence and lust held undisputed sway" (GC, pg 282). It was Napoleon who saw the wisdom of reopening the churches for Christian worship, and that, against the opposition of almost all his colleagues. **Out of the ruins of the Reign of Terror and the Revolution arose Napoleon Bonaparte to guide the tumult to his own elevation, place himself at the head of the French government, and strike terror in the hearts of nations.** It was **Napoleon who sent his general Berthier into Rome February 1798 to take the pope captive, thus bringing to an end the period of papal supremacy.** Rev 13:10, Dan 11:40

C. In Rev 11, we corroborate our conclusion above that France, the king that broke the papal power, "spiritually is called Sodom and Egypt" (vs 8) - for in it was manifest the overmastering licentiousness of Sodom and the atheism of Egypt. **Therefore, the spiritual king of the south in Dan 11:40, who brought to an end the dark period of papal supremacy in 1798, was France.**

III. And the king of the north shall come against him like a whirlwind, with chariots and with horsemen, and with many ships; and she shall enter into the countries, and shall overflow and pass over.

A. We notice in our discussion in part I above that the king of the south merely pushed at the papacy and did not conquer or destroy her. Since Rome was the last power introduced to have conquered the king of the north, the papacy must necessarily be that king next introduced in the narrative. **This prophecy thereby forecast wars between the king of the north - Spiritual Babylon, and the king of the south - Spiritual Egypt in whatever future form she may manifest herself - atheism, communism, secular humanism.**

B. The scripture describes a healing process to take place after the papacy received an apparent deadly wound at the hands of atheistical France. **"And I saw one of his heads as it were wounded to death; and his deadly wound was healed: And all the world wondered after the beast."** Rev 13:3
    1. In 1929 Mussolini restored the political status of the Papacy when he returned Vatican City to papal ownership.
    2. In Rev 13:11-17, we learn that **the United States will play a key role in giving life to the papacy by making an image to the papacy and causing the earth and them that dwell therein to worship her, whose deadly wound was healed**. The first evidence of the fulfillment of this prophecy paved the way for the fulfillment of the last part of Dan 11:40. **On January 23, 1984, Newsweek Magazine carried the story of Ronald Reagan's appointment of William Wilson to be the Ambassador to the Holy See.** The story began with these words: **"More than 200 years ago, John Adams predicted that the United States would never send a representative to the Holy See or permit 'an ecclesiastical tyrant' from the papal diplomatic corps to sully American soil.** Adams was a good Protestant but a poor prophet: Last week the White House and the Vatican announced they had established full diplomatic relations, thus consummating a courtship the Papacy has been quietly pushing for a century." The article closed with these words: **"For the pope, diplomatic recognition provides full access to a superpower in his quest for world peace."** In Time Magazine we read, no pope in modern times has taken such a direct interest in wielding diplomatic influence as John Paul. Now that the U.S. has become the 107th nation with which it has diplomatic relations, the Vatican may move to establish ties with the world's other superpowers. **It was January 19, 1984 upon the orders of U.S. President Ronald Reagan and the Holy See, the central government of the Roman Catholic Church, represented by the holy father, Pope John Paul II, full diplomatic relations were established between the two entities.** There have been consular relation with the Papal States, whose capital is in Rome, Vatican City, since 1797; but never before an ambassador to the Holy See. Such an announcement gave full recognition to the unique international sovereign role of the pope and his government, not only in Vatican

City State, but throughout the world where they exercise their spiritual and political authority. This diplomatic union **strikes a blow at the very principles upon which the United States of America is founded - civil liberty and religious liberty & the separation of church from the state** - because the "Holy See is the composite authority, jurisdiction, and sovereignty vested in and exercised by the pope and his advisors in the temporal and spiritual direction and guidance of the Roman Catholic Church throughout the world. The Holy See, consequently, is a moral entity, in modern terms, it is the central government of the Roman Catholic Church ." SC page 22-26

3. What brought these two powers together is what is called **"the commons enemy strategy."** In essence, Pope John Paul told U.S. President Ronald Reagan: **"Though we may not have a lot in common between us, we do have a common enemy in Communism. Let's work together for its downfall." Thus was born what Time Magazine called "the Holy Alliance."**
Time Magazine February 24, 1992
Thomas P Maledy, the official ambassador to the Holy See from 1989 to 1993 outlines how this struggle played out with a common enemy factor. "Both the U.S. and the Holy See faced the same powerful opponent. The years following World War II, when the Soviet Union acquired superpower status, were especially difficult for the U.S. and the Holy See. Both were deeply involved from 1945 to the late 1980s in efforts to thwart the advance of atheistic communism...... Senior Vatican officials told me on several occasions that the world owed a great thanks to the U. S. for having orchestrated and played a leading role in the collapse of the Soviet Union, and having done this in a nonviolent way ...." **Communism fell in 1989.** So what will the future bring? Ambassador Melady concludes: **"I believe that the U. S., as the only superpower, and the Holy See, as the only world-wide moral political sovereignty, have significant roles to play in the future. Their actions will impact the lives of people in all parts of the globe.** SC Chapter 4; Rev 13:11-18

4. **In June 1996, John Paul oversaw the establishment of diplomatic relations between the Holy See and Israel,** ending a tense standoff that had existed ever since 1948.

5. The January 1996 Inside the Vatican magazine listed the pope's travel plans for the year with trips to Central and South America, France, and other countries and noted there is an additional journey the pope longs to make to Jerusalem, in preparation for the Great Jubilee of the year 2000. The trip would include stops in Nazareth, Bethlehem, Mt. Sinai, and perhaps also in Cairo and Damascus. The pope is also expected to fix dates for the three continental synods of bishops for the Americas, for Asia, and Australia. SC 47, 51, 52, 137

   "He shall enter also into the glorious land, and many countries shall be overthrown" (Dan 11:41). "And all the world wondered after the beast" (Rev 13:3). Thus has the papacy gone forth to fulfill the prophecy of Dan 11:40-43

IV. **The final issue in the papacy's march toward world dominance is worship.** And all that dwell upon the earth shall worship him. Rev 13:8

   A. **In May 25, 1995 a Papal Encyclical Letter was issued entitled Ut Unum Sint, which in Latin translates to That They May be One** It was given as John Paul's commitment to ecumenism. There are 1.8 billion Christians in the world, about one third of mankind. A little over one billion are Roman Catholic, more than 300 million are Eastern Orthodox, about 100 million belong to the 'classic' Reformation churches and the rest are part of the maddening diverse and rapidly growing world of Evangelical Protestantism. The other growing and assertive religion on the world stage is Islam with about a billion adherents. The Catholic Church under John Paul II has been working hard to develop a non-confrontational relationship with Islam as we together cross the threshold of the third millennium. But the first order of business is Christian Unity, or ecumenism. As the second millennium has been one of christian division, so John Paul says that the third millennium must be one of christian unity. The division between the Christian West and the Orthodox Church of the East dates from 1054, while the division between the West issued from the 16th Century Reformation. The Catholic Church and the Orthodox Church are in essential agreement on doctrine, sacraments, and ministerial order. There are substantial disagreements in doctrine, sacraments, and ministerial order between Rome and the Protestant West. Ut Unum Sint declares that in Catholic teachings, the pope, as bishop of Rome, is successor to Peter, and that this Petrine ministry belongs to all Christians, whether they recognize it or not. In other words, the pope is the head of all Christian churches whether or not they recognize his leadership.

B. **Rome declares that the understanding of the gospel of justification is what caused the rift or separation of the Protestant churches from the Roman Catholic Church:** They claim that there are 2 sides to this gospel: The objective side, and the subjective side.
  1. The objective content is the person and work of Jesus - who He is and what He accomplished in His life.
  2. The subjective content is the question of how the benefits of Christ's work are appropriated and applied to the believer.
  The Reformers taught that we are justified by faith alone. Faith is the soul instrumental cause for our justification. In other words, we receive all the benefits of Christ's work through putting our trust in Him alone.
  Romes response to this at The Council of Trent (1545-1563) declared that a person can have faith and still not be justified. How so? The Council said that God does not declare a person righteous unless the person is righteous. This means that justification depends on a person's sanctification. **By contrast, the Reformers said justification is based on the imputation of the righteousness of Jesus, that the only grounds by which a person can be saved is Jesus' Righteousness, which is reckoned to him when he believes. The Council of Trent declared justification by faith alone to be anathema - an outrage, an abhorrence, a disgrace, and an evil. Trent declared that justification is accomplished through 7 works** called sacraments - baptism, confirmation, eucharist (communion), penance (confession/reconciliation), matrimony, holy order (priesthood), anointing of the sick (extreme unction) - necessary for salvation, though not every sacrament necessary for every individual. **According to Trent sacraments are efficacious signs of grace instituted by Christ and entrusted to the Church by which divine life is dispensed to us. In other words Rome determines who receives the benefits of Christ holy life and sacrificial death.** To assent to what the Reformers were teaching would be to undermine the very priestcraft and

ministry that Rome put in place to supplant the Priesthood and Ministry of Christ and rob the world of the knowledge and truth of His ongoing work of atonement. **This is the gospel according to Rome - fallen human beings, who themselves are in need of a Savior, claiming that which is the prerogative of deity alone, to forgive sins and punish dissenters. Then, claiming the right to compel men to accept their teachings by any means necessary, or be consigned to damnation and destruction.** Think you that those who concocted this supposed gospel know what they were doing? Unequivocally yes, otherwise, they would not have withheld the Scriptures from the people for nearly 12 long centuries while aggrandizing themselves at their expense. **The Word of God is as a light shining in darkness to expose error, falsehood, and all that is a counterfeit to its history, doctrines, prophecies, and revelations.** Nevertheless, after 50 years of collaboration between the Lutheran World Federation and the Roman Catholic Pontifical Council Promoting Christian Unity, The Joint Declaration On the Doctrine of Justification (JDDJ) was birthed, signed, sealed, and delivered in 1999 before crossing over into the third millennium, and is the vehicle by which ecumenism is rapidly expanding the reunification of Protestants and Catholics. **Is this a mere healing of the rift and end of the Reformation, as they claim, or is it the fulfillment of Rev 13 in which the apparent deadly wound is healed and the whole world wonders after the beast?**
Dan 8:11, 12, 23-25; Rev 13:3, 4, 7, 8, 11-17

While pushing hard to achieve her objectives, "**tidings out of the east and out of the north shall trouble him:** Therefore he shall go forth with great fury to destroy, and utterly to take away many. And he shall plant the tabernacle of his palace between the two seas in the glorious holy mountain; yet he shall come to his end, and none shall help him" (Dan 11:44, 45; Rev 14:6-12).

Chapter XXII

DANIEL 11 PART 6

SPIRITUAL BABYLON PURSUING WORLD DOMINANCE AND WORSHIP ENCOUNTERS SPIRITUAL ISRAEL, & THE CHURCH TRIUMPHANT

I. Who Reads The Warning Given By The Fast Fulfilling Signs of the Times?
   A. "The world is stirred with the spirit of war. The prophecy of the eleventh chapter of Daniel has nearly reached its complete fulfillment. Soon the scenes of trouble spoken of in the prophecies will take place. **Soon the battle will be waged fiercely between those who serve God and those who serve Him not.** Soon everything that can be shaken will be shaken, that those things that cannot be shaken may remain" (Test 9 14-16).
   B. While Spiritual Babylon is pushing hard to achieve her objectives, **"Tidings out of the east and out of the north shall trouble her: Therefore she shall go forth with great fury to destroy and utterly to take away many"** (Dan 11:44).

II. In order to understand the nature of this war, **we must look to the literal national, historical type so that the spiritual antitype may be clearly seen.**
   A. **As a result of Israel's sin and rebellion in falling before Satan's pagan sun worship, God raised up the Assyrians to remove the 10 tribes from before His face as a nation.** Failing to learn the lesson from beholding their sister nation's demise, **Judah and Jerusalem pursued a similar course and God suffered them to be removed from their land and be put under subjection to Babylon,** His chosen vessel to take the sovereignty the earth and to subdue all nations (Jer 25:9-12). After 70 years of captivity, God's promise was, "I will visit you, and perform My good word toward you, in causing you to return to this place" (Jer 29:10-14).
   B. **That men might know that the deliverance of Israel from Babylonian captivity was in His providence and judgment and not by the power of human ingenuity or machination, God surnamed Cyrus over 100 years before his birth as His agent, the anointed of God, to perform His pleasure** (Isa 45:1-4; 44:28).

   He further indicated that after 70 years were accomplished, He would punish the king of Babylon, and that nation for their iniquity, ..., and make it a perpetual desolation. Jer 25:12; TGEP p 51
   1. **And at the time appointed God called His people out of Babylon:** "Remove out of the midst of Babylon and go forth out of the land of the Chaldeans" (Jer 50:8). "Flee out of the midst of Babylon, and deliver every man his soul: Be not cut off in her iniquity; for this is the Lord's vengeance; He will render unto her a recompense" (Jer 51:6).
   2. **"The Lord hath raised up the spirit of the Medes: For His device is against Babylon**, to destroy it; because it is the vengeance of the Lord, the vengeance of His temple" (Jer 51:11).

   Tidings out of the east and the north foreshadowed trouble for the Babylonians. "Who raised up the righteous man from the east." The Lord **"raised up one from the north and he shall come:** From the rising of the sun shall he call upon Thy name (Isa 41:2, 25; 45:1, 13; Jer 50:1-3, 9; Dan 8:4, 20).

   "That saith of Cyrus, he is My shepherd, and shall perform all My pleasure: Even saying to Jerusalem, thou shalt be built; and to the temple, thy foundation shall be laid" (Isa 44:28).

3. **God further told how Babylon would be taken.**
   "O thou that dwells upon many waters (The Euphrates) abundant in treasures, thine end is come." Jer 51:13
   "A drought is upon her waters; and they shall be dried up."
   "I will loose the loins of kings, to open before him the two-leaved gates; and the gates shall not be shut" (Jer 50:38, Isa 45:1-3). Cyrus turned the River Euphrates that flowed under the outer wall and then between the the outer and inner wall the full length of the city. In the inner wall were huge gates of brass which, when closed and guarded, debarred all entrance from the river bed to any of the streets that crossed the river. Had the gates been closed at this time of festive revelry, the soldiers of Cyrus would have marched into the city along the river bed and marched out never getting beyond the inner wall. But knowing of an upcoming festival during which the whole city would be engaged in drinking and reveling, Cyrus had his army dig channels in advance, then, on the night of revelry, divert the river and make his attack. All that was foretold by the prophets of God was fulfilled that fatal night: **The waters were dried up, the gates were left open, and the soldiers of Babylon were so drunken that they forbore to fight.** Jer 50:38; 51:36, 39, 57, 30 By the time that Belshazzar (Bel-shar-uzur) realized what had happened, it was too late to save the kingdom. That night of dissipation cost the Babylonians their kingdom and their freedom. DR42-48, TGEP Chapter 3.

   > *Had the gates been closed at this time of festive revelry, the soldiers of Cyrus would have marched into the city along the river bed and marched out never getting beyond the inner wall.*

4. **The time of God's vengeance upon Babylon was also the time of Israel's deliverance, and the promise was:**
   "I will bring it health and cure, and I will cure them, and will reveal unto them the abundance of peace and truth. And I will cause the captivity of Judah and the captivity of Israel to return, and will build them, as at the first. And I will cleanse them from all their iniquity, whereby they have sinned and whereby they have transgressed Me" (Jer 33:6-8).
   "In those days, and in that time, saith the Lord, the iniquity of Israel shall be sought for, and there shall be none; and the sins of Judah, and they shall not be found: For I will pardon them whom I reserve" (Jer 50:20).

"In those days shall **Judah be saved, and Jerusalem shall dwell safely: And this is the name wherewith she shall be called, The Lord Our Righteousness"** (Jer 33:16).

III. **To the literal, national, local things pertaining to Israel and her enemies we find a spiritual antitype in the last days** by the principle of the double application or the principle of the first and the last mention. **This is the typology principle.** 1 Cor 10:11, Rom 15:4

   A. **That Spiritual Babylon, the papacy, is the power represented as being troubled by the tidings out of the east and out of the north has been clearly set forth in Dan 11 Part 5.** ` Positioning herself politically by establishing diplomatic relations with over 107 nations, including the USA, she presses toward world dominance, waging war against atheism in the form of communism. With the fall of communism in 1989 she ascertains that the way is clear to pursue **her ultimate objective in world dominance - worship.** Extending the invitation to Christians of all persuasions to join in her efforts toward unification, **she marvels at how readily many Protestants and Eastern Orthodox reach across the abyss that has separated them to make ecumenism a success.**

   B. **Israel represents Spiritual Israel, the Christian Church, at the time of the end:** Those who receive and accept the light of truth that God sends and orders their lives in harmony with it at whatever cost to themselves.

   C. **Cyrus is a type of Christ**, the LORD'S SHEPHERD, the LORD'S ANOINTED, the Righteous Man from the east, whose right hand the the LORD holds up, to subdue nations before Him, and rule over kings. Isa 44:28, 45:1, 41:2, John 10:11 Heb 13:20, 21, 1:6-13, Ps 2 When the heavens are opened and **Christ descends in clouds of glory from Mt Zion, the City of the Great King, on the sides of the North,** He is called **Faithful and True,** and in righteousness He comes to judge and to make war. His eyes are as a flame of fire, and on His head are many crowns;...... And He is clothed with a vesture dipped in blood: and His name is called **The Word of God.** And out of His mouth goes a sharp sword, that with it He should smite the nations: and He shall rule them with a rod of iron:...... And He hath on His vesture and on His thigh a name written, **KING OF KINGS, LORD OF LORDS.** Rev 19:11-16

1. We are further told that **as lightning comes out of the east, from the rising of the sun, and shines even unto the west; so shall the coming of the Son of Man be.** Matt 24:27

D. **What tidings go before the Lord** to prepare the way for His return, with which He smites the nations and troubles Spiritual Babylon?

1. **The tidings that herald the imminent return of Christ to take vengeance on Spiritual Babylon and for the deliverance of His people are depicted as coming out of the east and out of the north:** In Rev 14 we have the picture of the 144,000 who stand through the last crisis of earth's history - a time of trouble such as never was since the genesis of this world, proclaiming the last message of warning to be given to the world just before Christ's 2nd Advent. They are seen on Mt Zion with Christ, having the Father's name written in their foreheads. They sing a song of victory, and are called the first fruit unto God and unto the Lamb. Rev 14:1-5 Having introduced this victorious group, John next retraces the history of the work and experience that qualified them to be in this number. Here we discover that to them was committed the last messages of warning to be proclaimed before the close of human probation. **There are 3 distinct messages which could only be proclaimed after we entered the time of the end, the time beyond which Christ could return.** This period was entered in February 1798. It is evident that these messages are designed to prepare us for the Advent because immediately following them is the depiction of Christ's return and the reaping of the earth's fully ripe harvest. Rev 14:6-20. These are messages which God gave unto Jesus Christ, which He sent and signified by His angel (depicted as 3 angels flying in the midst of heaven), who gave it unto His servants the prophets, who gives it unto the church, who in turn gives it unto the world. Hence, **the message proceeds** from the same place as does Christ when the heavens are opened - **from Mt. Zion, the City of the Great King, on the sides of the <u>North.</u> The tidings that trouble the king of the north are depicted** in Rev 7:1-4 **as ascending out of the east. Those who believe, love, and live out the principles of truth** unfolded by them **are** depicted as **being sealed by God** to stand through the time of trouble and indignation in the great day of God's wrath when human probation closes. They are **called the 144,000.** In Joel, they are depicted

as blowing a trumpet in Zion, and sounding an alarm in God's holy mountain, that the inhabitants of the land may tremble. In bearing their message, the 144,000 are described as **a great people and strong; the likes of which there has never been, nor shall be after them.** They shall **run like mighty men; climb the wall like men of war.** The earth shall quake before them; the heavens shall tremble: **And the Lord shall utter His voice before His army:**.... For He is strong that executed His Word: For the day of the Lord is great and very terrible; and who shall abide it? Rev 6:14-17, 7:1-4, Dan 12:1 Joel 2:1-11

IV. **Spiritual Babylon is exposed and her battle plans laid bare before the people; and in her fury she goes forth to utterly destroy and move out of the way those who bring these tidings.** And God reveals the activity that is taking place in heaven and upon the earth in His messages (GC 606-611).

    A. **At a time when men in the political, economic, educational, and secular world want to remove the religion of Christ** from their institutions, the message is given in trumpeted tones (Isa 58:1)

"**Fear God, and give glory to Him; for the hour of His judgment is come: And worship Him that made the heaven, and the earth and the sea, and the fountains of waters.**" This message calls the inhabitants of earth to return to the worship of the living God, who created the heavens and the earth and all that in them is in 6 literal days, and then set aside and blessed the 7th day in honor of and as a memorial of His work of creation - a day in which He calls men aside for special communion and fellowship with Himself, the Lord God, our Creator. **Why? Because in love Christ would have every man, woman, and child know that He is carrying forward His final work of atonement which involves a work of judgment to determine those who will be the subjects of His everlasting kingdom.** As we entered the time of the end, February 1798, many of Jesus parables have specific application admonishing His follower to watch for His return. Mark 13:32-37 sets forth 4 watches in which His followers are to watch that they may know where we are in the stream of time and what we must do to prepare for His return. This is the 1st of 4 watches in which the 1st of 3 angels messages began to sound, announcing in a special since that God's judgment hour is come. It began to be preach from the fall of

1833 to the fall of 1844, and is the antitype of the memorial of blowing of trumpets. Dan 11:31-35, 12:4, 6, 7, Lev 23:23-32, Rev 14:6, 7 **As literal Israel was to repair the breach made in the earthly sanctuary by Babylon under Nebuchadnezzar after 70 years captivity when God called them out of Babylon, so Spiritual Israel is to repair the breach made in the heavenly sanctuary by Spiritual Babylon (the papacy) who had set up her own priest- craft and ministry and robbed the world of the knowledge and truth of Christ priest hood & ministry and His ongoing work of atonement.** Isa 44:28, 45:13, Ezra :1; 6:1-15; 7:21-27; Isa 58:1, 6-14, Dan 8:11, 25, 2 Thes 2:1-4

B. From the summer to the fall of 1844 the Midnight Cry was proclaimed towards the end of the midnight watch, Oct 22, 1844. Matt 25. **"And there followed another angel, saying, Babylon is fallen, is fallen, that great city, because she has made all nations drink of the wine of the wrath of her fornication"** (Rev 14:8). By virtue of their rejection of the 1st angels message and the message of the coming of the bridegroom, the majority of Protestant churches rejected the giver of these messages. In turning away from this advancing light of the Reformation, that God caused to shine forth from the books of Daniel and Revelations, they chose to continue in the darkness of ignorance of present truth. Consequently, they have no knowledge of the way into the heavenly sanctuary nor understanding of the ministry and work of Christ Jesus there. Their fall, which began in 1844 (Rev 14:8) will not be complete until they have fully retreated back to the **intoxicating errors, falsehoods, superstitions, traditions, and customs of Spiritual Babylon.** Then the angel of Rev 18 will come down with great power decrying the fallen condition of Babylon, lightening the earth with his glory, and preparing the way for God's final call to His people to come out of Babylon before the judgment of the plagues.

C. **"And the third angel followed them, saying with a loud voice: If any man worship the beast and his image, and receive his mark in his forehead, or in his hand, the same shall drink of the wine of the wrath of God, which is poured out without mixture into the cup of His indignation;** and he shall be tormented with fire and brimstone in the presence of the holy angels, and in the presence of the Lamb: And the smoke of their torment will ascend for ever and ever: And they have no rest day nor night, who worship the beast and his image, and whosoever receives the mark of his name. **Here is the patience** of the Saints: **Here are they that keep the commandments of God, and the faith of Jesus.** And I heard .... **Blessed are the dead which die in the Lord from henceforth:** ...... **that they may rest from their labors; and their works do follow them."** Rev 14:9-12, Chp 15 Here is recorded the most dreadful threatening ever communicated to mankind. Ever before this, God's wrath has been tempered with mercy, but not in this threatening. **In giving his warning the third angel contrast those who receive the mark of the beast with those who keep the commandments of God.** Wrath and indignation will be the reward of the former, blessings the latter. How vitally important than that we understand and know what constitutes the beast, his image, and his mark. It is a matter of eternal damnation or eternal life. Chapter IX Sec II & III identifies the activity and mark of the beast; and Chapter XI identifies the beast.

As human probation nears its close and Jesus is about to end His high priestly ministry in the Heavenly Temple, another angel is sent to add his voice to the third angel; and he cries mightily and with a strong voice swells the 3rd angels message to a loud cry that the earth may be lightened with his glory:

1. **He announces the full and complete fall of Babylon,** which began in 1844, and has continued to the extent that it has **"become the habitation of devils, and the hold of every foul spirit, and the cage of every unclean and hateful bird." And have made all nations drunk with her falsehood, errors, and superstitions of Babylonian sun worship.** Rev 18:1-3
2. Then comes the final call to come out of Satan's counterfeit of the religion of Christ: **"Come out of her, my people, that you be not partakers of her sins, and that you received not of her plagues."** Rev 18:4
3. At some point during this conflict, **Spiritual Babylon - The The King of the North - will "plant the tabernacle of her palace between the 2 seas in the glorious holy mountain."** What could this possibly have reference to?
    a. An ex Jesuit has said that Rome has always wanted to move the seat of the empire from the 7 hilled city of Rome to Jerusalem. This scenario is unlikely because, at this point in the prophecy, we have transitioned from the literal to the spiritual interpretation. Jerusalem was destroyed in AD 70 along with the earthly

temple which ceased to be God's temple in the earth AD 31 with the cruxifixction of Christ.

b. With the transition from the literal to the spiritual came the transition from the earthly to the heavenly sanctuary as the center of Christ's mediatorial work in behalf of human beings. In this mediatorial work, God only accepts the service of love, and love cannot be forced or compelled.

Therefore, **God, not only grants but preserves the free will of the governed, and He rules by their consent for Him to be enthroned in their minds and hearts. Thus, the temple of God in Heaven extends to include the body temple of every free moral beings where He sits enthroned through His Spirit:**

"What? Know you not that your body is the temple of the Holy Ghost which is in you, which ye have of God, and ye are not your own? (1 Cor 6). **"Know ye not that ye are the temple of God, and Spirit of God dwelleth in you? If any man defile the temple of God, him will God destroy; for the temple of God is holy, which temple ye are.** I Cor 6:19; 3:16, 17

With the entry of sin, the Spirit of God was dethroned from the body temple of man, self took His place, and selfishness took the place of love. **God's plan of redemption, salvation, and recovery from the ruin of sin involves man's spiritual regeneration in which the Spirit of God is again enthroned in the body temple by the willing consent of the redeemed.** When self is enthroned, man has no power to resist the will of Satan to whom he gave his allegiance in rebelling against the will of God. **What God achieves by love" and the preservation of the will, Satan seeks to do by coercion and force in destroying the will.** His agent in these last days, the papacy, to whom he gave his seat, his power, and great authority, stands on record as hating the idea of the free moral agency of man, of man's liberty of conscience.

During the period of papal supremacy, called the Dark Ages, by withholding the Scriptures from the masses, she not only controlled the will of the people, but exercised blatant control over the will of the state, requiring all to bow down to her dictates. In the fulness of time, God resurrected His

Word right in the heart of Catholicism, and marched His people out from under the darkness of her superstitions, falsehoods, errors, traditions, customs, and oppressions: Thus giving her an apparent deadly wound. Rev 13:1-10

However, this apparent deadly wound is to be healed, and the whole world will wonder after her and worship her. She will again seek to be enthroned in the temple of God to control the will of the masses - the church and the state. Called "the man of sin" and "the son of perdition," her leader will oppose and exalt "himself above all that is called God, or that is worshipped; so that he as God sitteth in the temple of God, showing himself that he is God" (2 Thes 2:2-4).

This cannot be the heavenly temple, and therefore, must be the body temple of men where God alone is to be enthroned, which constitute the spiritual glorious holy mountain. This will signal the close of human probation, and the commencement of the events of Dan 12:1 and Rev 16:1-21, in a time of trouble such as never was since there was a nation. This will lead to the drying up of the spiritual River Euphrates - the peoples, nations, multitudes, and tongues that uphold Spiritual Babylon - to prepare the way for Christ's second advent (Rev 17:15).

There will then be a threefold union formed in which the whole world will be joined together by the spirit of devils working through the king of the north, Spiritual Babylon, and all false systems of religion found controlled by the dragon, the beast, and the false prophet, united for an all-out battle against Christ and His followers who bring the last tidings of mercy and warning to a fallen world, in the battle of Armageddon. Then, Spiritual Babylon shall come to its end, for the Lamb shall overcome them: "For He is Lord of lords, and King of kings: And they that are with Him" - the called, and chosen, and the faithful - shall be delivered.

The seas represents the peoples, multitudes, nations, and tongues in both spheres of the earth - the Old World and the New World. Dan 11:44-45, Rev 12:3, 4, 13:1-10, 11-17, 16:13-16, 17:10, 13-15

Chapter XXIII

DANIEL 12 PART 1

THE CLIMAX - EVENTS SURROUNDING CHRIST'S 2ND ADVENT

I. **When Human Probation Closes!**
   A. "And at that time shall Michael stand up, the great prince which standeth for the children of thy people: and there shall be a time of trouble, such as never was since there was a nation even to that same time: and at that time thy people shall be delivered, everyone that shall be found written in the book" (Dan 12:1).
   1. **What time is here brought to view?**
      The time to which we were brought in Daniel 11:45
      "when the king of the north - Spiritual Babylon - shall plant the tabernacles of his palace between the two seas in the glorious holy mountain." This may be when Spiritual Babylon shall sit enthroned over all peoples, multitudes, nations, and tongues in the spiritual temple of God where His Spirit alone should be enthroned by the willing consent of His people, from the Old World to the New World. Rev 17:1, 3, 15, 18, 13:8, Dan 11:45, 1 Cor 3:16, 17
   2. We have shown in our study on Dan 11 Part I that Michael is Christ, the Prince of the Covenant, our Prince and Savior.

3. **But, what does it mean for Michael, or Christ to stand up?**
   In our study of the Sanctuary - Chapter XIII to XVI, we saw that **when Christ ascended to Heaven in AD 31, He sat down "on the right hand of the throne of the Majesty in the heavens; a minister of the sanctuary and of the true tabernacle, which the Lord pitched, and not man"** (Heb 8:1, 2). As our High Priest, Christ invites us to "come boldly unto the throne of grace, **that we may obtain mercy, and find grace to help in the time of need"** (Heb 4:16). Here, the prophet represents **the 2 phase ministry of Christ to secure for His people the forgiveness and the blotting out of sins confessed and repented of, which ministry are for our justification and our sanctification.**
   When Christ ceases this work the destiny of every child of humanity will have been decided, for **the last phase involves a work of investigation and judgment to determine those who shall be the subjects of His everlasting kingdom.**
   Chapter 15, Part III.
   Since the sitting down of Christ points to the commencement of His final work of atonement in a two phase ministry, the standing up must point to the end of His High Priestly ministry in the heavenly sanctuary and the close of human probation. Dan 12:1

4. **What is this time of trouble such as never was since there was a nation, and when may it be expected to occur?**
   The time of trouble is signaled to occur and will take place after Michael stands up, which is when Christ ceases his high priestly ministry in the heavenly sanctuary and human probation closes. This time of trouble is associated with and may be understood to be that experienced by the nations. It is not to be confused with the period of great tribulation referred to in Matt 24:21, 22. That tribulation came upon the church and points to the persecutions during the 1260 years of papal supremacy. Never before nor since has the church been subjected to such oppression and wholesale slaughter in which believers were burned alive, buried alive, and tortured to death beyond the limits of human endurance. The time of trouble is not about religious persecution of God's faithful followers, but of international calamity and disaster that comes upon

the nations when Christ ceases to intercede in behalf of guilty humanity. Will God's people be persecuted during this time? Yes, but not to their martyrdom or destruction. "When Christ leaves the sanctuary, darkness covers the inhabitants of the earth. In that fearful time the righteous must live in the sight of a holy God without an intercessor. The restraint which has been upon the wicked is removed, and Satan has entire control of the finally impenitent. God's long-suffering has ended. The world has rejected His mercy, despised His love, and trampled upon His law. The wicked have passed the boundary of their probation; the Spirit of God, persistently resisted, has been at last withdrawn. **Unsheltered by divine grace, they have no protection from the wicked one. Satan will then plunge the inhabitant of the earth into one great, final trouble**" (GC, pg. 614).

He will then lead those under his control to accuse "those who honor the law of God" "of bringing the judgments upon the world, and they will be regarded as the cause of the fearful convulsions of nature and the strife and bloodshed among men that are filling the earth with woe." (GC, pg. 613, 614). Satan has no more regard for the wicked who are under his control, than he has for the righteous, whom he hates, because they honor God and keep His commandments. He will use the disasters and international calamity, to intensify the spirit of hatred in the wicked, to persecute the righteous. This will plunge the people of God "into the scenes of affliction and distress described by the prophet as the time of Jacobs's trouble," a time of wrestling with God - to deny self, to agonize before God, to pray long and earnestly for His blessing (GC, pg 621). God's people will be agonizing with Him for the assurance that their sins have gone before in confession and repentance and have been overcome; praising God for His goodness, mercy and love in reclaiming them as His own; claiming the promises of God for their preservation in the time of trouble (Ps 27; 46; 91; 121).

God permits this affliction and distress to come upon the righteous that they may be purged of the final droughts of earthliness so that they may perfectly reflect His character. His judgments do not initiate or cause the calamities and disasters of the time of trouble. However, when "the decree issued by the various rulers of Christendom against commandment keepers shall withdraw the protection of government and abandon them to those who desire their destruction" (GC, pg. 626), "God's judgments will be visited" (GC, pg. 627) upon them in the wrath of the 7 last plagues "just before the deliverance of His people" (GC, pg. 627; Rev 16). "The nation with which He bears long, and which He will not smite until it has filled up the measure of its iniquity in God's account, will finally drink of the cup of wrath unmixed with mercy (GC, pg 627).

"And at that time thy people shall be delivered, everyone who shall be found written in the book" (Dan 12:1). **This final time of trouble concludes with the deliverance of God's people.**

The book in which they are found written is the book of life. As a result of Christ's work in the investigative judgement and His final work of Atonement, they are found worthy to have their names eternally enshrined therein. Dan 8:9-14, 21, 26, 27; Rev 13:8, Chapter IX, Part IV - A & B.

II. A Special Resurrection of Both the Righteous and the Wicked.

A. **"Many of them that sleep in the dust of the earth shall awake, some to everlasting life, and some to shame and everlasting contempt"** (Dan 12:2). This resurrection will take place between the time when Michael stands up and when His people are delivered. It is one of three resurrections brought to view in the Scriptures, and is often missed or overlooked. To distinguish it from the others, we shall examine the two general resurrections described in the Scriptures - one in which **all the righteous** are raised, and the other in which **all the wicked** are raised. **"Marvel not at this: for the hour is coming in which all that are in the graves shall hear His (Michael's) voice and shall come forth; they that have done good, unto the resurrection of life; and they that have done evil, unto the resurrection of damnation."** One is called the resurrection of life, the other the resurrection of damnation. John 5:28, 29. Acts 24:15

In I Thes 4:13-16 we find that the resurrection of the righteous takes place when Christ "descends from heaven with a shout, with the voice of the archangel, and with the trump of God."

Revelation 20 tells us that there is 1000 years between the resurrection of the righteous and the resurrection of the wicked. Satan will be bound to the earth during this time having no one to tempt. The finally impenitent perish in the brightness of Christ coming, while the living righteous are caught up and changed following the resurrection of the righteous dead, ever to be with the LORD. After the 1000 years, when Christ and the righteous return to the earth, the wicked will be resurrected, and Satan will be loosed, having subjects to tempt. The resurrection of the righteous is called the first resurrection, and the resurrection of the wicked is called the second resurrection. Rev 20:1-8

Since only the righteous are raised in one of these general resurrections, and only the wicked are raised in the other, these cannot be the resurrection referred to in Dan 12:2 in which many (not all) of both the righteous and the wicked are raised.

Christ alluded to this special resurrection in the gospels when He told His persecutors **"Hereafter shall ye see the Son of Man sitting on the right hand of power, and coming in the clouds of heaven."** Matt 26:64, Mark 14:62 In order to see Him coming, they must be raised before He makes his descent. **"Behold He comes with clouds; and every eye shall see Him, and they also which pierced Him." Rev 1:7** It is believed that this resurrection takes place when the voice of God is heard announcing the day and the hour of Christ return. Rev 16:17, Mark 13:32, Dan 12:2

III. A Call to Teach

A. **"They that be wise shall shine as the brightness of the firmament; and they that turn many to righteousness as the stars forever and ever"** (Dan 12:3).

This takes place in these last days, in this time of the end when "perilous times shall come." "For men shall be lovers of their own selves, covetous, boasters, proud, blasphemers, disobedient to parents, unthankful, unholy, without natural affection, truce breakers, false accusers, incontinent, fierce, ... heady, high-minded, lovers of pleasure more than lovers of God; having a form of godliness, but denying the power thereof" (2 Tim 3:1-5).

"Some shall depart from the faith, giving heed to seducing spirits, and doctrines of devils" (1 Tim 4:1).

Those who teach the truth as it is in Jesus will uphold:

- **The prophecies which tell us where we are in the stream of time.**
- **The principles of the free moral agency of man: Liberty of conscience above the legislation of civil powers, and the authority of the Word of God above the visible church.**
  These 2 principles constitute the fundamental principles of Protestantism.
- **Health reform**
- **Sabbath reform and the binding claims of God's holy law.**
- **The priesthood & ministry of Christ Jesus in the heavenly sanctuary and the truth of the atonement.**

These are they who shall shine as the brightness of the firmament; and …… as the stars forever and ever as they reflect the character of Christ in thought, in word, and in deed, and in habitual practice.

IV. **A Book of Prophecy Sealed and Shut up Until the Time of the End.**
   A. **"O Daniel, shut up the words, and seal the book, even to the time of the end: Many shall run to and fro, and knowledge shall be increased." Dan 12:4**
   Certain portions of the prophecies of the book of Daniel were sealed not to be understood until we entered the time of the end. As we saw in our study on Dan 11:33-35, we entered the time of the end at the end of the 1260 years of papal supremacy in February 1798.
   At this time, an explosion in knowledge in general was to be expected, and in particular in the Bible. With the conscience of man freed from the encroachments of an apostate church seeking only to aggrandize itself at the expense of humanity; and freed from the shackles of papal superstitions, errors, falsehoods, traditions, and customs, the world has witnessed an explosion in knowledge in communications, transportation, the sciences, and technology in 200 years that puts to shame the accumulated advancements made during the 1260 years of papal oppression known as the Dark Ages.
   Thus, the prophet has taken us over the events from when we entered the time of the end to the end of time, when there shall be time no longer for fallen humanity to bear sovereign sway over the heavens and the earth. **And the world as we know it shall come to a climactic end.**

Chapter XXIV

DANIEL 12 PART 2

A SEALED BOOK UNTIL THE TIME OF THE END

I. The Book of Prophecy Sealed and The Words Shut Up, Until The Time of The End "O Daniel, shut up the words, and seal the book, even to the time of the end .... How long shall it be to the end of these wonders?
And I heard the man clothed in linen, which was upon the waters of the river, when He held up His right hand and His left hand unto heaven, and swear by Him that liveth for ever that **it shall be for a time, times, and an half; and when he shall have accomplished to scatter the power of the holy people, all these things shall be finished."** Dan 12:4-7.
   A. What book is here sealed, and the words shut up, even to the time of the end? No doubt, it is portions of the book that he wrote bearing his name, Daniel, the culmination of which is outlined in chapter 12.
     In this book, Daniel - called, chosen, and anointed of the Lord as His prophet - received a series of visions, revelations, and prophecies of events from his time to the end of human history when Christ sets up His everlasting kingdom. In these revelations, God discloses the rise and fall of universal empires, the final disposition of sin and sinners, and the reward of the righteous. **By the principle of enlargement through repetition, the Lord gave the prophet a complete revelation of events to transpire to the close of human probation, the time of**

national calamity, the special resurrection, and the deliverance of His people.

1. The secrets which the wise men, the astrologers, the soothsayers, the magicians, the sorcerers, and the Chaldeans could not make known unto king Nebuchadnezzar, the Most High God made known unto His humble servant Daniel. At times, the prophet was troubled, perplexed, and grieved in spirit, but he kept the the matter in his heart. At other times, Daniel fainted, was sick certain days, was astonished at the vision, and did not understand it. Thus did the prophet seek the Lord his God by prayer and supplication, with fasting, sackcloth and ashes, to learn of the hidden, secret things, to clear up perplexities, to ascertain the true meaning of the vision, and get understanding, until he is told to "shut up the words, and seal the book."

B. **"How long shall it be to the end of these wonders? .... It shall be for a time, times, and an half; and when he shall have accomplished to scatter the power of the holy people, all these things shall be finished."** Dan 12:7

In the response to the question about the wonders addressed in part A, **it is significant that the answer given singles out the period of papal supremacy, and thus the papal power.**

1. From the time that Satan, working through Pagan Rome, gave to Papal Rome his seat, his power, and his great authority, the papacy has been **the principle agent of Satan to war against Christ and His church.** Rev 13:2

   This activity of Rome, following its transition from its pagan to its papal phase, is set in a definite time period of 1260 years which corresponds to the time, times and half of time. This period was **the height of papal oppression but not the end of its influence or activity, for the whole world shall yet wonder after her when her apparent deadly wound is healed.** We are thus cognizant of the fact that in addition to being set in a definite time frame of 1260 years, which brought us to the time of the end, **the activity of Rome is also set forth in an indefinite** time **period,** which will take us to the end of time: **"And when she shall have accomplished to scatter the power of the holy people, all these shall be finished."** Dan 12:7, Rev 13:7-10

2. The above analogy being correct supports our conclusion that **the papacy is the power who shall plant the tabernacle of her palace between the seas in the glorious holy mountain; yet, she shall come to her end, and none shall help her.** " Dan 11:45, Rev 17:16-18, Dan 7:11 **This action of the papacy will signal the close of human probation** as Michael stands up to end His High Priestly Ministry in the Heavenly Sanctuary, and the end of time breaks forth upon an unprepared world in a time of trouble such as never was since there was a nation to that same time, which ends with a special resurrection, followed by the deliverance of God's people.

> " the papacy is the power who shall plant the tabernacle of her palace between the seas in the glorious holy mountain; yet, she shall come to her end, and none shall help her. "

C. In Dan 12:7 and Rev 10:5 we see a picture of Christ standing upon the waters and upon the earth with His hands outstretched to heaven declaring, in Daniel time prophecies of events which were yet future in a definite and indefinite time frame; and in Revelation declaring the end of definite prophetic times, thus bringing to view the fulfillment of the 2300 day/year prophecy. SM 2, page 108, BC 7, page 971

II. Who Shall Understand?

Daniel heard, "but understood not," and again inquired "**what shall be the end of these things?**" Once again the Lord said, "Go thy way, Daniel : for **the words are closed up and sealed till the time of the end.**" Many shall be purified, and made white, and tried; but the wicked shall do wickedly: and none of the wicked shall understand; but the wise shall understand" (Dan 12:8-10).

A. Though Daniel did not understand, he was told that the vision would be understood at the time of the end when the 1260 years of papal supremacy would end in February 1798.

B. To further establish His people in the vision, additional prophetic periods are cut out of the 2300 years. "**And from the time that the daily (paganism) shall be taken away, and the abomination that maketh desolate (the papacy) set up, there shall be a thousand two hundred and ninety days. Blessed is he that waiteth, and cometh to the thousand three hundred and five and thirty days.**"

As we have seen in our study of Dan 11 Part III, the time of the taking away of paganism is not the same as the time of the establishing of the papacy. For the taking away of paganism we look to the year 508 when a mighty crisis had ripened between Catholicism and the pagan influences still existing in the empire. The year AD 508 marked the beginning of the 1290 year prophecy, which period ended the same year as the 1260 year prophecy, February 1798. Noting that the Scriptures introduce the 1335 year prophecy in relationship to the 1290, by pronouncing a blessing on those who wait and come to it, we conclude that the two prophetic periods have the same starting point. This point is supported by the fulfilled prophecy in Rev 10:5-11, in which the little book, corresponding to the sealed portions of Daniel's prophecies, is opened, giving to those who came to it a blessed experience likened to the sweetness of honey in their mouth. Since the expiration of both the 1260 and the 1290 time prophecies brought us to the time of the end, we understand why they were used to answer the question "how long shall it be to the end of these wonders" (Dan 12:6, 8).

The blessing of the 1335 year prophecy would be realized by those who waited and came to the year from the spring of 1843 to the spring of 1844.

One of the errors made in the reckoning of the 2300 year prophecy was reckoning its starting point from the spring of 457 BC, in which the last year of the prophetic period would be from the spring of 1843 to the spring of 1844. This error in reckoning is what led to the blessing of the 1335 prophecy, which was the belief that Christ would come before the end of year to gather them to Himself in the clouds of glory, ever to be with Him. This is the blessing likened unto the sweetness of honey in Revelation 10: 5-11. But, it was not to last, **for after the blessing of the 1335, the angel told Daniel**

"But go thou thy way till the end be" (Dan 12:13). John's experience after taking the little book out of the angel's hand was: "I took the book out of the angel's hand, and ate it up; and it was in my mouth sweet as honey: and as soon as I had eaten it, my belly was bitter." **Then John was told, "thou must prophesy again before many peoples, and nations, and tongues, and kings"** (Rev 10:10, 11).

III. **The End of the 2300 Year Prophecy**

"How long shall be the vision, the daily (paganism), and the transgression of desolation (the papacy), to give both the sanctuary and the host to be trodden underfoot? .... Unto two thousand three hundred days; then shall the sanctuary be cleansed."

A. In all the prophetic discourses that were set in a definite time frame preceding Dan 12:13, we had not come to the end of the 2300 years. It is this verse that brings us to this end, **"when Daniel shall stand in his lot at the end of the days."** The end of the days has specific and definite reference to the end of that prophetic period which began this entire study of prophetic time in Dan 8:13, 15.

   1. **Every other time prophecy is cut out of the 2300 years: The 490 year prophecy, which is broken up into 49 years, 434 years, and 7 years; the 1260 year prophecy; and the 1290 year prophecy which extends to the 1335 year prophecy having the same starting point.**

   2. This end of days is also **portrayed in Rev 10:6, and is represented as the end of prophetic time when "there shall be time no longer,"** and it culminates in two bitterly disappointing experiences for the people of God - one following the blessing of the 1335 years, and the other following the midnight cry of the summer & autumn 1844 during the midnight watch (Mark 13:32-37).

B. Thus we are brought to the time when Christ, our Great High Priest, has entered upon His final work of atonement in the heavenly sanctuary, and the closing events surrounding His 2nd advent are to take place. It is here that God's people received the message from God **"Thou must prophesy again before many** peoples, and nations, and tongues, and kings" (Rev 10:11, 11:1).

It is here that we entered the indefinite time period - "and when he shall accomplished to scatter the holy people, all these things shall be finished" (Dan 12:7). No definite time prophecy extends beyond the 2300 year prophecy. No future event or message to the people of God is set in a definite time frame beyond October 22, 1844, when the 2300 year prophecy ended.

REFERENCES

Anti Christ 666 (AC-666) — Roy Allan Anderson

New Age and The Illuminati (NAI) — Roy Allan Anderson

Patriarch and Prophets (PP) — Ellen G. White
Prophets and Kings (PK) — "
Desire of Ages (DA) — "
Acts of the Apostles (AA) — "
Great Controversy (GC) — "

Early Writings (EW) — "

The Great Empires of Prophecy (TGEP) — A. T. Jones

Daniel and the Revelations (DR) — Uriah Smith

The Cross and the Shadow (CS) — Stephen Haskell

Sundays Coming (SC) — G. Edward Reid

Selected Messages 2 (SM2) — Ellen G. White

Council on Diets and Foods (CDF) — Ellen G. White

Bible Commentary 7 (BC 7) — SDA Church

The Two Babylons (TTB) — Alexander Hislop

Complete Works of Flavius Josephus (CWFJ) — Flavius Josephus

The Decline of the Roman Empire Vol II (DRE) — Edward Gibbons

Bible Reading for the Home (BRH)   **SDA Church**

Certainty of the Three Angels Messages (CTAM)   **Louis B. Ware**

All Scriptures from The Authorized King James Version

TEACH Services, Inc.
P U B L I S H I N G

We invite you to view the complete
selection of titles we publish at:
www.TEACHServices.com

We encourage you to write us
with your thoughts about this,
or any other book we publish at:
info@TEACHServices.com

TEACH Services' titles may be purchased in
bulk quantities for educational, fund-raising,
business, or promotional use.
bulksales@TEACHServices.com

Finally, if you are interested in seeing
your own book in print, please contact us at:
publishing@TEACHServices.com

We are happy to review your manuscript at no charge.

www.ingramcontent.com/pod-product-compliance
Lightning Source LLC
Chambersburg PA
CBHW062012180426
43199CB00034B/2488